Stellar Spiral Notebook Stories:

A Collection of Inspirational Short Stories

recorded by Ina May Wrye

DORRANCE
PUBLISHING CO
EST. 1920
PITTSBURGH, PENNSYLVANIA 15238

Dorrance Publishing Co
585 Alpha Drive
Pittsburgh, PA 15238
Visit our website at www.dorrancebookstore.com

ISBN: 979-8-89211-079-2
eISBN: 979-8-89211-577-3

Dear Reader:

If you gave me a title and asked me to write a short story about the subject, I would be hard-pressed to complete the requested assignment, but sometimes I feel the Holy Spirit's guidance so intently that I have to pick up a pen and start recording the revealed words in a spiral notebook or on a scrap of paper if my notebook is not available. My writing process reminds me of how years ago a secretary took dictation from the boss. Thus my completed stories seem to me to be stories recorded by me as revealed to me rather than stories written by me.

Therefore, as you read these little stories, I pray that the Holy Spirit reveals to you His will for your life.

Prayerfully,
Ina May

Acknowledgements

Scripture references, unless otherwise undisclosed are taken from the King James Version (KJV) of the Bible. Scripture quotations marked The Living Bible (TLB) are taken from the Living Bible, copyright 1971 by Tyndale House Foundation. Used by permission of Tyndale House Publishers, Inc., Carol Stream, Illinois 60188. All rights reserved.

The Notebook

On New Year's Day, 2019, I stared at my 2018 Mother's Day gift—a Stellar Spiral Notebook—given to me by my daughter, Diana. When she gave me the notebook, she stated she knew I enjoyed writing and wanted me to record some of my stories. As I flipped through the eighty-page notebook, I felt a sense of pain. All the pages were blank. I had not written one thought, story, or inspiration in almost eight months. Yes, I had some notes for three or four stories, but I hadn't carved enough time from my hurried schedule to write the words in the requested notebook.

The pain of my failure to record these "precious memories" for my daughter was intensified by the fact that I had seen a similar notebook before. In fact, when I realized my mother's memory was fading, I had given my dear Momma a journal on Mother's Day 2000 to record her reflections of her life, but when I found her journal while I was cleaning her house in 2006 after her death, the pages of her journal were blank, too.

Over the years, I have come to realize how difficult it is for women to find the time to do all the things that they need to do. God gave me peace about "being enough" as I wrote these words:

"Being Enough"

I will never be able to do all the things that I need to do, but I will be able to do enough to make a difference. God does not require perfection. Do the best that you can, and it will be enough.

Dear Lord, thank you for giving me peace about "being enough" and reminding me "your grace is sufficient for me."

Reference: "Be not weary in well doing" (2 Thessalonians 3:13b).

Limited Edition

On a whim, I baked a batch of homemade chocolate chip cookies for my daughter's housewarming gathering—a celebration of the beginning of a new chapter in her life. A new chapter she was starting not necessarily by choice but of necessity as she said goodbye to a fifteen-year broken marriage.

As the last pan of cookies cooled, I searched for the perfect platter to display the cookies. In the utility room, I noticed my old red-and-blue pure Quaker Oats cookie tin. It was a little worn from years of use but still had some useful years left, I thought. As I opened the empty tin, I smelled the aroma of cookies left from years past. As I savored the Heavenly scent, I turned over the tin and noticed embossed on the bottom of the tin: "Limited Edition 1983." I smiled. Nineteen-eighty-three was a wonderful year for me since it was the year our daughter was born into our home. We had a boy in 1980 and our girl in 1983; we felt our family was now complete.

My daughter, always remember that you are our one-of-a-kind "1983 Limited Edition." We love you, and we are so very proud of you.

And to all the daughters whose mothers have already gone and who may be feeling a little worn and maybe a little used from years of usefulness, may you always remember you are a one-of-a-kind "Limited Edition." God loves you, and He is so very proud of you.

Reference:

"I will praise thee; for I am fearfully and wonderfully made" (Psalm 139:14a).

The Little Pack of Tissues

After a yoga class in October 2017, my friend and I were enjoying a relaxing lunch, visiting and catching up with what our kids were doing, when I got the sniffles. You know what I mean. I couldn't find a tissue fast enough. As I was digging a crumpled tissue from the bottom of my purse, my friend handed me a little pack of tissues. I said, "I've got it taken care of," but she insisted that I take the little pack of tissues.

I remembered what my Momma once said: "If someone gives you a gift, regardless if you think you need it or not, say 'Thank you' and accept their gift."

So I said, "Thank you," placed the little pack of tissues in my purse, and went on enjoying our lunch.

May 2018, three funerals later—including my husband's mother, I was still carrying around the little pack of tissues, but now the little pack of tissues was at the bottom of my purse.

Late May on an early Monday morning, I started to work; the tire indicator light on my car came on. *No big deal,* I thought, because the temperature had fluctuated from yesterday's high of 65 degrees to this morning's low of 35 degrees. The indicator was giving me a false reading, but I stopped my car, got out of my car in the dark, kicked my four tires to be sure they were inflated, and drove on to work. I thought, *I'll go at lunch to the tire store and have the tires checked to be sure there is not a problem with my tires.* Work was extremely busy and I didn't find the time to have my tires checked, so I drove home after an eleven-hour workday.

That night when my husband called from Kentucky, he stated, "You need to get your tires checked," after I told him my car's tire indicator light was on. He reminded me our daughter had not had her tires checked when her indicator light came on, and she had a flat tire on busy Briley Parkway. Thank God a "Good Samaritan" helped her change the tire or that situation could have been a disaster.

"Okay. Okay. You're right. I'll get my tires checked," I said.

For two more days, I repeated the same course of action and had the same conversation with my husband at night.

When I woke up Thursday morning, my inner voice said, *What is wrong with you? Get up and go get your tires checked.* So I got up early, dressed, checked that my tires were still inflated as I verified by kicking each tire—a procedure I had done for the seventh time in four days—and hurriedly drove to the tire store with my car's tire indicator light still on.

Arriving at the tire store, I told the owner, also my second cousin, my tire indicator light was on and asked him to check my tires. As I flopped into the first available chair in the service waiting room, I thought, *What a waste of time on my day off!* After a few minutes, I moved to another seat because the radio speaker was over my chair and the radio was too loud for my tired ears. Two other customers joined me in the waiting room. The man sat quietly. The woman and I spoke and exchanged pleasantries about the weather. After a while the woman started talking. She said, "I buried my husband a week ago."

I sympathetically replied, "I'm sorry for your loss. How long were you married?"

She replied, "Forty-six years." She went on to say her husband had been in good health; he had never been sick. In fact, about a month ago they took a family vacation; all their children and grandchildren were able to go with them. A few days before the vacation was over, "My husband became sick. We all thought he had caught a bug and it would pass. When we got back home, he was still sick. He went to his doctor, he had tests, and he was diagnosed with cancer. The doctors told him if he had treatments it wouldn't help him to live longer, so he decided to not have treatments. He lived approximately a month after the diagnosis; he had time to say goodbye to all of us and plan his funeral."

She continued on. "My husband was older than me, so he had retired. I continued to work my twelve-hour days. When I came home at night, he would be watching old Westerns on an old Magnavox TV. I tried to buy him a new updated TV, but he didn't want one. I would cook our supper, take his plate of food to him as he watched his Westerns, and take my food to another room to watch my shows on another TV." She went on to express other feelings of regret bordering on guilt.

Finally, I stopped her and said, "You were married forty-six years to the same man; that is love. You worked long hours so he was able to retire and do what he wanted to do—watch old Westerns on an old TV; that is love. Due to you continuing to work, you were able to finance a dream vacation for your entire family; that is love.

"In fact, I understand your comments about your husband watching old Westerns while you still worked because that is what is happening at my home, but I received some insight into my situation. When my husband was a child, his family didn't have a TV. They had farm chores, including milking cows twice a day by hand. Occasionally, they went to a neighbor's house and watched Roy Rogers on a black-and-white TV. What a treat that was! So the pleasure of retirement for my husband is and your husband was watching the old Westerns and other reruns that they missed as children because they had to work on the farm to help support a large family. Our contribution is that we continued working so they could enjoy their retirement and relive part of their childhood that they missed.

"So when you come home to a silent, lonely house after working a long day, prepare your supper. Before you go to your TV room, stop and turn on the old Magnavox to a Western in remembrance of your husband, and go on living your life. Enjoy your children, grandchildren, and your work."

As I finished talking, the woman started crying. Tears streamed down her face that I'm sure had been bottled up for weeks trying to be strong for her family. She desperately needed a tissue. Instinctively, I reached for my purse, pulled out the little pack of tissues from the bottom of my purse, and gave the little pack of tissues to her.

She said, "Thank you."

My cousin walked over to me and said, "Ina May, your car is ready. You had a nail in your tire. No charge for the repair."

I thanked him and left the tire store realizing after driving around with a nail in my tire for days, God had sent me to the tire store with a little pack of tissues that had been gifted to me by a friend seven months earlier.

The next day, I carried lunch (AKA homecooked meal) to my two cousins who work at the tire store, thanking them for my free tire repair. I spoke briefly about yesterday's conversation with the woman.

My cousin said, "I thought you two knew each other by the way you were talking."

I said, "No, I had never met her before. You know, she buried her husband a week ago."

He said, "Yes, I know. He was a good man!"

I told my cousin I felt Divine Intervention had sent me to the tire store on Thursday because I'm not a risk taker and always have had my tires checked when the indicator light comes on. Since my daughter had a flat tire recently on a busy road, it was freshly on my mind how dangerous a flat tire can become. The fact that I drove for four days with a nail in my tire without a disaster happening was miraculous.

He agreed.

Christmas Fudge

In January 2019, two days before my husband's birthday, I stared at him eating a remaining piece of fudge from a Christmas tin. After I had made the fudge for Christmas, I selected this particular tin because of the label on top: "Merry Christmas to Lorene Wrye from First Baptist Church, Lebanon." As I read the label, I realized this would be our first Christmas without my husband's mother, Lorene Wrye. Mrs. Wrye always made fudge for her family at Christmas, and placing my fudge in her Christmas tin would be my tribute to her.

I'm not sure what year Mrs. Wrye started the Christmas fudge tradition at the Wrye home, but like most traditions sometimes events occur that fall short of *Hallmark* moments. As the story was told to me by Mrs. Wrye years ago, because she was busy and didn't know if she would have time to get everything done at Christmas she made her fudge weeks ahead, placed the fudge in a tin, and hid it on top of the refrigerator so her children wouldn't find it. At Christmas she retrieved the tin of fudge from the top of the refrigerator, opened the tin, and discovered it was almost empty; she demanded to know who ate the fudge. Reportedly, her husband, Archie, fessed up. One night he was hungry when he came in from the barn after milking cows. He knew where Lorene had hid the fudge. So he got the tin down, had a piece, and shared the fudge with his four hungry boys. This happened several more times until the fudge was almost gone. When Mrs. Wrye realized it was her husband, Archie, who had been eating the fudge and sharing it with the boys, she calmed down and all was forgiven.

A decade passed and my husband was serving in the Air Force, stationed in Thailand during the Vietnam War. Being away from home, especially at Christmas, is never easy. A lot of letters were written during the time he was away from home, as verified by the stack of letters that were saved by my husband's mother. "Precious letters" she saved, even when she downsized from the family home to an apartment, were found in her possessions after she passed. Christmas 1968, my husband's mother sent a tin of Christmas fudge to him in Thailand.

"How did that fudge taste after being shipped so many miles in a tin?" I asked.

"It tasted like home—good," he replied.

In 2007, when my husband and I moved to Kentucky, he discovered we had black walnut trees on our farm. That fall we picked up the black walnuts, hulled, dried, cracked, and picked out the nuts from the shells. At Christmas my husband asked me to make fudge that year for his Sunday School class. Over the years, the number of people that have received Christmas fudge from us has expanded. In 2018, I made five batches of fudge in order for everyone to have a taste. I asked myself, what makes the fudge recipe on the back of the marshmallow creme jar so special? Is it the chocolate, sugar, butter, marshmallow creme, evaporated milk, or vanilla? Maybe it's our family's secret ingredient, black walnuts (instead of English walnuts or pecans) that have always grown on our farms and have been available to us free of charge because we were willing to harvest and process them. Maybe, but I think the fudge is special because as you are eating a square of the delicious fudge you are reminded that you are loved.

As my husband closed the lid on his mother's Christmas tin, I asked him, "How many pieces of fudge do you have left?"

"Two small pieces," he replied.

I thought, *You have been rationing your fudge—making it last longer than usual.* I said, "You know, I have enough ingredients left to make another batch of fudge."

He didn't answer me.

I said to myself, "Sounds like a nice birthday present for you.... I can almost smell the chocolate melting!"

The Christmas Fudge Recipe

3 cups sugar

3/4 cup butter or margarine

1 small (5-ounce) can evaporated milk (about 2/3 cup)

12 ounces semisweet chocolate chips

1 jar (7-ounce) Kraft marshmallow creme

1 cup chopped black walnuts

1 tsp. vanilla

Line a 9-inch square pan with foil, with the ends of the foil extending over the sides. Bring the sugar, butter, and evaporated milk to a rolling boil in a large saucepan on medium heat, stirring constantly. Cook for 4 minutes or until the candy thermometer reaches 234 degrees F, stirring constantly. Remove from heat.

Add chocolate and marshmallow creme; stir until melted. Add nuts and vanilla; mix well.

Pour into the prepared pan; spread to cover the bottom of the pan. Cool completely. Use foil handles to lift the fudge from the pan before cutting into squares.

My God Is an Awesome God

Life at its best is often stressful in today's modern world, but some unexpected change can occur and life's stress can be raised to a whole new level. Twenty-seventeen started out rather routinely, but by spring the direction of the wind shifted and my world became harsher. With summer came yet one more change at work. The wind blew harder. Fall arrived without any relief in sight, as more responsibilities were added to my workload. I could feel the stress building inside my body as I tried to meet expectations and push on facing the bitter wind.

After a swim on Thursday, November 2nd, I noticed a small red spot along my left hairline. I dismissed my concern thinking my swim cap must have irritated my skin. On Saturday, I noticed the spot was still there; I checked the internet for medical advice, but my search was fruitless. On Sunday, I felt fine and went to church. On Monday morning, the spot had spread down my forehead; I felt as if I were coming down with the flu. I told my husband, "I've got to go to the doctor; this might be shingles." I checked in as a walk-in at my busy doctor's office. The receptionist told me my doctor didn't have any appointments; he was triple booked. I agreed to see the first available nurse practitioner, thinking if the NP couldn't figure this out he could ask my doctor for his input. The NP took one look at my face and said, "You have shingles." I was devastated, realizing shingles can be serious. I asked him if I had caught shingles from one of my patients, who had them three weeks ago. I thought to myself, *She actually died from complications of the shingles since the virus went to her brain.*

The NP said, "No, you have shingles because you had chickenpox as a child, you're over sixty, and you're stressed."

You sure nailed that diagnosis, I thought.

He went on to say, "I'm going to give you an antiviral medicine. If you break out in your eye, go to your eye doctor immediately because you can lose sight in your eye from having shingles."

The wind blew briskly as I picked up my medicine at the pharmacy. I went home and went to bed. I started taking the medicine around the clock to get the medicine in my system. That night I was in agonizing pain; it felt like my eye socket was on fire. I went to the bathroom and looked in the mirror. The right side of my face was perfectly normal; the left side looked like someone had taken a baseball bat to my face—it was bright red and my eye was almost swollen shut. I pried my left eye open with my fingers and realized the shingles had broken out on my eyelids. I was devastated realizing the left side of my face might never match my right side again, and it looked as if I were facing the loss of vision in my left eye. I felt the urge to cry, but I stopped myself. I thought, *I can't cry; it might make the virus on my lids spread to my eye,* I went back to the couch in agony.

As I lay there suffering, I thought, *The devil is really enjoying my pain; I bet he is laughing like a hyena.* Then I remembered a little song my daughter, Diana, sang as a teenager: "Our God Is An Awesome God." I was not physically able to sing, hum, whistle, or speak the words to the song, but my soul sang: *"My God is an awesome God, He reigns from Heaven above with wisdom, power and love. My God is an awesome God."* The second time through, I felt something overshadow me. I was aware that something physically had changed inside my body. I felt better. I smiled as I sang, in my mind, the song for the third time. I peacefully drifted off to sleep. The next morning when I looked in the bathroom mirror, I realized the shingle lesions had stopped at my eyelids. I had no new places on my body and the existing ones started to heal. In a few days, I was able to return to work, physically looking a little rough but spiritually at peace knowing God had healed me. I felt a sense of peacefulness as the winds of my life calmed once more, but the reprieve was short lived.

December 3rd, Sunday morning, I woke up with what I thought was a migraine because my vision was blurry. I took an Advil, drank a cup of coffee, and went back to bed. Normally, my migraines last about twenty to thirty minutes, but this one didn't go away. I told my husband I couldn't see well enough to go to church and stayed in bed. All day Sunday my vision continued to not be exactly right. I told my husband, "First thing Monday, I've got to go to my eye doctor." He drove me to Nashville on Monday to the eye doctor's office. The technician who did my preliminary screening said, "There is nothing wrong with your vision. You can see with each eye okay."

As she left the room, I thought, *I had better tell the eye doctor specifics about how I am seeing before he starts the exam.* I said, "I can see fine with my left eye and fine with my right eye, but when I use both eyes my vision is blurry."

He checked my vision and confirmed my diagnosis. "Your eyes are not focusing together," he stated.

I thought, *I went back to work too soon after having the shingles to my heavy computer workload; I have strained my weak left eye, and I have gotten my vision out of focus.* His solution was to send me to another specialist, who added lines to my left glasses' lens to help train my eyes to focus together again. When I left the specialist's office, I noticed very little improvement in my vision. I had to be off from work for another period of time.

Basically, I had my walking-around vision with both eyes, but I had to use either my left or my right eye if I wanted to see clearly.

On December 8th, my mother's birthday, I received my first Christmas card from my childhood pastor and his wife. The Christmas card said: "This season may you see and know that God still loves you."

"Thank you, God, for that encouragement, because this vision problem is taking longer to correct than I expected," I said to myself. In the meantime, my husband drove me around, including to and from work, as I tried to go on with my life. I told him, "If my vision doesn't get better, I'm going to have to go on disability or retire early."

"Wait and see what happens," he said.

On December 18th, my children, husband, and I celebrated my birthday at my favorite restaurant. I ordered my favorite meal—the salad bar—and they ordered the same. What a happy day it was; I felt total joy in my heart, as I had realized while riding from work to the restaurant that my vision had returned. I told my family my vision was better. Leaving the restaurant, we paused in the parking lot. As we took a family selfie, I felt a pleasant breeze fluff my hair.

Going home, I told my husband, "You won't have to drive me to work in the morning."

"Are you sure?" he said.

I said, "Yes!" and to prove it to him I read the numbers on the truck gauges and street signs as we went home.

On March 7th, I went for my yearly checkup: no pain, my vision same as usual, and no disfigurement from having the shingles. My doctor said, "You are fortunate; I have another patient who lost vision in one of her eyes from having shingles.

Most patients suffer for years with burning pain, but you are pain free."

"Yes, I realize 'My Awesome God' is in the healing business and is with me whatever wind blows in my direction."

Reference: "And he saith unto them, 'Why are ye fearful, O ye of little faith?' Then he arose and rebuked the winds and the sea; and there was a great calm. But the men marveled, saying 'What manner of man is this, that even the winds and the sea obey him!'" (Matthew 8:26-27).

The Key to Heaven Was Hung on a Nail

After my Daddy died, I realized he knew he almost missed Heaven. Even though Daddy believed in God, he was bitter toward God since He had taken his beloved son, David, at age nine in a farming accident. At the age of seventy-eight, while Daddy was reading the Bible to Momma due to her Alzheimer's disease, the Holy Spirit convicted him as he read Mark 16:16. Daddy realized he had never accepted Jesus as his Savior. Daddy asked Jesus into his heart and life; he stated he had to be baptized in obedience to God and he was, on May 25, 2005, at Fall Creek Baptist Church with his family, including Momma, in attendance.

Daddy died September 25, 2007, but in that brief twenty-eight months Daddy witnessed and quoted scripture to everyone, including a preacher who came to visit him. He just wanted to be sure everyone he knew was saved.

On a Thursday in the spring of 2007, I was at Daddy's house—the home of my childhood. I sat down on the worn-out couch after I finished doing all my weekly chores. Daddy started talking. "People today don't believe there is a real Hell. To them it's like a hot August day—just a little uncomfortable. To me in my mind, Hell would be like I fell on that wood stove there, wrapped my body around it, and was stuck there forever and ever burning with no relief in sight. If people really grasped what Hell is going to be like, they would be more concerned about their souls, their loved one's souls, and everybody-they-came-in-contact-with's souls."

Five years passed. As I was running errands during the week before Easter in 2012, I kept passing a local church that had a message on their sign: "The Key to Heaven was hung on a Nail." As I drove past the church sign, it was as if I could hear the nails being driven into Jesus' body. By chance, I had a small burn on my hand that throbbed with pain every time I touched it against something. I was reminded of the words Daddy had spoken about Hell years ago. I went home, sat down, and started writing as if I were taking dictation. The result was the words to "The Key to Heaven Was Hung on a Nail." Even though I describe myself as a one-talent piano player, I sat down at the piano and played the melody to the song.

The Sunday before Easter, April 1, 2013, I asked our song leader, George Thomas, if I could sing a song. He looked at me in disbelief. He thought I was pulling an April Fool's joke on him, because I had told him before I had a choir voice and was not a soloist, but when the Holy Spirit pricks one's heart one has to do what God has laid on his or her heart. As I sung the words acapella and my husband hammered three nails into wood between the verses, I felt in my heart that I had been obedient to what God had told me to do.

I have shared the words of the song with three talented singers, but no one has been inspired to do anything with the song. It may be like what my daughter said when I shared the song with her: "That sounds like one of those old gospel songs."

I said, "Thank you," but in my heart I knew that she was trying to tell me that my song was not contemporary enough for today's modern times, but in my heart I know God's message is unchanging and still needs to be shared.

Reference:

Mark 16:16: "He that believeth and is baptized shall be saved; but he that believeth not shall be damned."

The Key to Heaven Was Hung on a Nail

by Ina May Wrye

Verse 1
I hung the keys of my life on a nail by the door—
drug my weary feet across the floor.
I dropped in to my chair; as I breathed (pause)
the cold night air; I drifted off to sleep in my chair.
I dreamed about my keys to my home, job, and car
that hung on a nail by the door.
I realized one key of my life was not there
was the Key to Heaven that was hung on a nail.
Verse 2
I awoke with a start. (pause) I fell on my knees.
I asked Jesus to come into my heart.
Through my tears of joy, I saw the Key to Heaven
was hung on a nail there for me.
So now, I have the Key to Heaven that was hung on a nail.
Verse 3
The Key to Heaven was hung on a nail. He became your
sacrifice—paid your full price.
So today, please don't delay.
Accept the Key to Heaven that was hung on a nail there for you.
Chorus
So long ago, the Key to Heaven was hung on a nail.
For God so loved the world
He hung his Son there on a nail.

Whosoever believes in him will not go to Hell,

but will receive the Key to Heaven

that was hung on a nail.

Amen.

Sound effect: Nail being hit three times with a hammer at the end of each verse.

Through Adversities

Due to the Covid-19 pandemic, it had been over a year since I had my hair cut and my hair was showing it had been neglected. "Enough is enough," I said to myself as I masked up and went to get my hair cut.

As I sat in the young hairstylist's chair, she asked me what I wanted done to my hair. I showed her I needed six inches cut off my hair to remove the damaged ends. I said, "I'm thankful no one lit a match near my hair, because my hair's dry ends might have gone up in flames." She laughed. She then proceeded to comb my fine tangled hair. She left the tangles in the bottom half of my hair; she handed me a mirror to show me she planned to cut right above the tangles. I agreed.

As she cut my too-long-for-my-age hair, I said, "I'm glad you are able to be back at work." She agreed and went on to say that while she was off work due to the Covid-19 pandemic, she was able to go with her husband, who was a truck driver. "We went to states that I had never been to before, and I saw sights I had never seen before."

I said, "Sounds like you had a wonderful time." I paused and then added, "Sometimes through adversities, we receive unexpected blessings."

She agreed.

And once again, I was reminded that through my mother's adversity, Alzheimer's disease, Daddy saw the need to read the Bible to her. When he read Mark 16:16, the Holy Spirit pricked his heart, he accepted Jesus as his Savior, and in obedience to God he was baptized when he was seventy-eight years old.

Regrets

Recently, I tuned in to a classic Billy Graham Crusade service from 1988. The familiar comforting voice of the evangelist preached on the brevity of our time on earth; he emphasized that "life is shorter than we think."

No kidding, I thought. *I turned thirty-three years old in December 1988; now I'm carrying a Medicare card.*

Due to the restraints of time, he stated he regretted that he didn't study his Bible more when he was younger. He stated his "focus was on preaching the gospel during the crusades," but now he was spending more time "studying the Bible." He regretted "due to being away from home preaching in the crusades, I didn't spend as much time with my children when they were young. They turned out all right; all five are Christians and are preachers or serving in ministerial work." He noted, the "earthly credit" for their outcomes goes to "my wife, Ruth."

After my Daddy was saved and baptized at age seventy-eight by my childhood pastor (now a senior adult), he came to me with tears in his eyes. He stated he regretted that he didn't come to our home to visit with the family after my brother, David, died; he felt he had failed our family.

I quickly replied, "What are you talking about? There was nothing but an outpouring of love and support from the church and community after David passed. You were in seminary, working a fulltime job and pastoring our church on Sunday; you were doing all you could physically do at the time. You didn't come after David died in 1961 because the Holy Spirit didn't send you. Daddy was so angry and bitter toward God that He took David. If you had come to our home to visit at that time, Daddy may have cursed the Holy Spirit and never been saved. God sent you 'right on time' in 2005."

Billy Graham had regrets about not studying the Bible more when he was young and not spending more time with his children when they were young, but the Holy Spirit directed him to preach the gospel to millions through the crusades. When he was a senior adult, he had the time to study his Bible more and spend time with his children. Now that he has gone on to be with the Lord, the multitudes of souls that were touched by the Holy Spirit and saved during the crusades years ago continue the Lord's work.

There is a gospel song, "Right on Time," about Jesus not coming immediately when his friend Lazarus was sick. His friend died. His sisters didn't understand why Jesus didn't come sooner, but they still kept their faith. Then Jesus raised Lazarus from the dead, "Right on Time."

Sometimes we can't see with our earthly eyes God's plan for our life, but if we follow the Holy Spirit's direction like Billy Graham and my childhood pastor, we will always be "Right on Time" with God's will.

Our Dwelling Place

As my husband built our little cabin on our God-given farm in Kentucky, I snapped pictures of the construction progress starting with the hole dug for the ceiler. It was such a joy for both of us to watch the daily process. Finally, when the cabin was finished, I snapped a picture of the completed project. As I studied the photo of our cabin nestled among the trees after a snow, I thought, *This picture looks like the front of a Christmas card*. So that year, I used the picture to make our Christmas card and started a tradition of using a God-inspired picture to grace our yearly Christmas card, a tradition that has continued for years now. Often people say, "I always look forward to seeing what you do with your Christmas card each year," but I know in my heart that it is not my creative talent but the Holy Spirit guiding me.

On 8/20/2020, I read the comfort chapter of the Bible: "Let not your heart be troubled; ye believe in God, believe also in me. In my Father's house are many mansions; if it were not so, I would have told you. I go to prepare a place for you. And if I go and prepare a place for you, I will come again, and receive you unto myself that where I am, there ye may be also."

It took my husband and me a total of eight years to prepare and build our little one-bedroom cabin in Kentucky. One cannot comprehend what Jesus is preparing in 2000-plus years for us, His believers, but the sunset of 8/20/2020 was so spectacular that I felt the Holy Spirit stir the bowl of my soul as if I were viewing a microscopic glimpse into our future dwelling place with our Lord. So l instinctively started snapping pictures of our future home with Him.

Reference: See John 14:1-3.

On 8/20/2020, Bro Carl and Mary Lena Price celebrated sixty years of marriage; they credited the Holy Spirit for bringing them together and being with them through the years of their marriage and service to our Lord. Such words of wisdom from your faithful servants continue to inspire us.

The Tip

As I waited my turn to get my hair cut, I watched the elderly woman in front of me pay the young hairstylist. She received the senior discount, paid $13.00, and left no tip. "Ouch!" I said to myself as the elderly woman left the building with her middle-aged son. In my mind, I thought, *She probably no longer realizes that she should leave a tip, but her son could have left one.*

After the young hairstylist finished cutting my hair, giving me a more youthful hairdo, the young hairstylist said, "Senior cut – $13.00."

After I handed her a $20.00 bill, she handed me the change back. Then I handed her the $7.00 and said, "This is for you!"

She joyfully said, "Oh, thank you!"

Years ago, my son said, "If people can't give a generous tip to their waitress (who works hard for their money and depends on tips for a large portion of their living), they need to stay home and cook their own food."

Thank you, my son, for reminding me as I grow older by your words and deeds to be a generous tipper to individuals in the service industry.

Years ago, when our son still lived at home, he came home after work one day; as he walked in the door, he said, "I've lost my billfold."

"Oh, no," I said, thinking how difficult it would be to replace what he had lost in his billfold. As his Daddy and I asked him where he had been, he realized he had paid for a meal at Waffle House after work. Immediately, he drove back to the restaurant. When he entered the restaurant, the waitress that had served him earlier said, "After you left, I found your billfold on the floor; I put it up for you." She then handed him his billfold with everything intact.

After my son told me what had happened, I said to his Daddy, "Our son has always tipped his waitresses generously; looks like his generosity was returned to him today."

He agreed.

Home Safe

When my son was a newborn, I often found myself waking up at night for no reason and going down the hall to his room to look at him lying in his crib sleeping peacefully. It was as if someone was waking me up and telling me to double check that he was all right, even though I already knew he was sleeping safely in his bed in our home.

One afternoon as I was visiting Ma (my Momma's mother), I told her about my almost obsession that I needed to check that my baby was safe in his crib. She said, "If you ever feel led to check on your baby, do it." She went on to say, "When Christine and Corene were babies, I woke up in the night for no reason and went to check on them. Corene (my Momma) was sleeping peacefully, but I noticed Christine's skin had turned blue. I picked her up, she took a deep breath, and her skin started turning pink again."

"Oh, Ma!" I said. I realized if my Ma hadn't picked up Aunt Christine, she would have probably died as the result of SIDS (AKA crib death). I also realized God had been merciful to my Ma that she didn't have to experience the loss of a second baby, as she had lost one a few years earlier as the result of an accident.

My mother had told me about the loss of her older sister, Ernestine, as a baby, but Ma never mentioned her to me. I never asked Ma about Ernestine; I just seemed to sense that it was too painful for her to talk about, so I never questioned her about Ernestine's accident.

Our daughter joined our family in 1983; I continued my nightly safety checks when I was prompted to do so.

Almost too quickly, the teenage years arrived at our home with their own set of challenges. I tried to stay awake until our children came home at night, but exhaustion would overtake me and I would drift off to sleep. I would wake up in the early morning after midnight and before sunrise, go down the hall, and check they were home safe. When our children were away from home at night, I always kept a porchlight and lamp by the front door on. After our children came in, they would take their shoes off at the door and tiptoe down the hall to their rooms. Only a mother can know the relief of seeing by lamplight a pair of boots and shoes left by the front door, signaling her children made it home safe one more time.

It seems like a mother blinks, her children are grown, and they have moved out on their own, but that doesn't stop a mother's need to check that her children are safe.

On 1/19/2019, it had rained all day; the temperature was in the fifties, but the weather forecast was for freezing rain and snow before midnight. As my husband and I watched the weather, I said, "Diana's working late tonight. Maybe I need to text her and remind her to be careful driving home tonight." I paused and thought, *She's thirty-five years old, independent, and living in her own home; she might think my reminder text is nagging and helicoptering.* I sat in my chair wondering what to do. Time passed. I thought about what my Ma had said thirty-eight years ago about checking on your baby. I waited. I asked Diana's daddy, "What do you think about my sending a text to Diana about the changing weather?"

He said. "Do it!"

So I texted her, "If you are out tonight, be careful, watch for ice on the road since the weather is supposed to be colder, Love Momma." I went to bed early, but I awoke in the predawn hours. I checked my phone. I had a message from Diana at 11:05 P.M. "Home safe." As I read the words out loud, I thought "home safe" are two of the sweetest words a mother will ever hear.

2000-2007 were the last years my parents lived on the earth.

The last memory of seeing my parents walking together is etched on my brain. In fall 2005, I had been at my parents' home to bring their weekly meals, medicines, freshly laundered clothes, and groceries. After I gathered my things, I started carrying to my car dirty laundry, empty dishes, my purse, and garden vegetables my Daddy had given me. Momma followed me to the car to help me. Daddy came down the hill to retrieve her so I could leave. As they feebly helped each other walk together back up the hill to their home, I noticed their images. Daddy, 6-feet-plus with beautiful snowy white hair, and Momma, 5 feet 2 inches, with shining snowy-white hair, were now elderly—time was short. I fought back the tears as I paused to watch them until they were in their "home safe."

After Daddy passed on September 25, 2007, we buried him September 26, 2007, beside Momma at Fairview Cemetery. I took a walk that evening at sunset. As I faced west, I noticed two small clouds had drifted toward the sun. The two clouds caught my attention. One snowy-white cloud to the left was higher or taller than the snowy-white cloud to the right. The two offset clouds reminded me of my parents walking together toward their earthly home in the fall of 2005. As I ran to get my camera to snap a picture to capture the moment, I couldn't help but smile as I thanked God for my parents and His reassurance through these two offset snowy-white clouds in the sky that my parents' souls were now "home safe" with Him.

To my dearest children:

When I have breathed my last breath on this earth and have been laid at the foot of my Momma's grave at Fairview Cemetery in Norene, Tennessee, please know my soul is "home safe" with my Heavenly Father. Love you always, Momma.

The Dim Flashlight

Through the years, God has never provided a pillow of fire at night to guide me, spoken to me through a burning bush, or sent a choir of angels to deliver a message to me, but He has guided me daily through the Holy Spirit, spoke to me through the Bible or prayers, and delivered His message to me through my faithful Momma and other women of faith who not only talked the talk but walked the walk daily. These methods that God chose to communicate with me may not have been as dazzling or bright as a pillow of fire, burning bush, or angels. In fact, sometimes God used only a dim flashlight to illuminate my path.

Decades ago, when Momma and I began the drive to my cousin's home for a bridal shower, it was a pleasant late-afternoon summer day. The sun was shining brightly, the temperature was warm, but not too hot for our unairconditioned car. We made a stop two doors down from the Norene General Store to pick up my Great Aunt Era. She lived in a three-room shotgun-style home—humble by most standards, but elegant in my mind because she was an inspiration and blessing in my young life. As she got in the car in the backseat with me, I commented, "The pink blooms on your tree are so beautiful."

She said, "That's a Formosa tree; notice the leaves." I looked at the small leaves that looked more like hedge leaves than tree leaves. She said, "When we get back tonight after dark, they will be closed, but tomorrow they will open again." I was fascinated. Aunt Era was a natural teacher by the way she lived her life. She always had a kind word to say about everyone she had ever met; she was a woman of faith and always had time for a child.

We continued on our drive, passed the Norene General Store,

and headed south. After we went up a hill, we stopped at the second house on the right to pick up my paternal grandmother, Granny May. As Granny got in the car, she said, "I brought a flashlight since it will be dark when we leave the shower."

Onward we drove on Cainsville Road; we left Wilson County and entered Rutherford County. Unlike the rocky, hilly terrain of Wilson County, Rutherford County was flat and had fertile soil for farming. In about a mile or two, Momma turned right into my cousin's driveway. Her newly built home was set in the middle of a dairy farm. The perfectly mowed lawn, pasture for the Holstein dairy cows, and barn with silo were a perfect picture of rural life in America in the 1960s.

What a wonderful time we had at the shower. The delicious slices of decorated cake, mixed nuts, mints, and fruit punch tasted heavenly. The joy of watching the bride open her gifts, the laughter as we played party games, and the visiting with family and friends made time pass too quickly. Before I knew it, it was time to go home.

As we said our goodbyes and gathered our purses to leave, my Granny grabbed her trusty flashlight. When we got outside, it was dark. Granny turned on her flashlight. Instead of the expected bright beam of light, there was only the small bulb in the center of the flashlight burning dimly. My Aunt Era said, "Look, Ina May, Granny's flashlight looks like a lightning bug." We all laughed, including Granny, but surprisingly that little bulb provided sufficient light for all of us to see to safely get to the car without tripping and falling. It also aided my Granny to see how to get from our car into her home without an incident.

When we left Aunt Era at her home, I noticed the Formosa leaves on her tree had closed, signaling the end of another wonderful day.

Thank you, Dear Lord, for Christian women whose legacies continue to inspire us even after they are gone.

Reference: "Thy word is a lamp unto my feet, and a light unto my path" (Psalm 119:105).

A Bible that Is Falling Apart...

While sorting through my parents' home in the autumn of 2007, after they had both passed, I found among the fifty-nine years of accumulation several Bibles that were falling apart. Most of the Bibles I recognized as belonging to my mother but this particular old, ragged one, I didn't recognize.

As I continued the daunting task of sorting, I made three piles: save, give away, and throw away. The save pile was divided into three stacks—one for each of my brothers and me. As I looked at the old tattered Bible, I thought, *Why did Momma save this Bible? No one could possibly use this Bible—it's too fragile,* but I could not bring myself to place the old Bible in the discard pile so I laid it aside. As I continued to sort through my Momma's collectibles, clutter, and trash, the old tattered Bible seemed to draw me. I stopped my sorting, went back and picked up the old Bible. I opened the Bible to the presentation page and read the following exquisitely written penmanship: "Presented to Mrs. Mary E. Beadle by her mother on April 9, 1899." Over one hundred years ago my mother's great-grandmother gave her daughter a Bible. In awe, I realized I was holding my great-grandmother's Bible that my great-great-grandmother had given her.

From an early age, I knew my mother was a woman of faith by the life she lived daily, but now I knew she came from a long line of women of faith. I humbly hugged the old tattered Bible, placed it in the treasured save pile, and prayed, "May I continue to walk in the footsteps that you have left me to follow and continue to teach the next generation to follow in the footsteps of faith in God."

A Bible that is falling apart... means a life that isn't.

Steady Pace

While my older brother was hospitalized battling Covid-19 (in the fight of his life), he stated during one of my numerous phone calls to him, "I have a nurse that reminds me of Momma. I don't mean that she looks like her; she moves like her—not too fast or too slow. She just keeps a steady pace or speed."

Since our Momma was able to cheerfully complete her workload and help others, I always thought of her as being a fast worker, but in reality my brother was right. Momma maintained a "steady pace."

Momma was always up before sunrise and everyone else in her household. In the winter, she would start the fire in the wood stove from the coals left from the night before. Then she always prepared a country-style Cracker Barrel-type breakfast for her family. She viewed cereal and milk as not an adequate breakfast for her family. In the summertime, for variety she sometimes cooked fried chicken (that she had processed from our farm), homemade biscuits, milk gravy made from the fried chicken drippings, fresh corn and sliced tomatoes from our garden, and blackberry jam that she made from blackberries that we picked on our farm. Breakfast was served early at her home; if you slept late, your breakfast was left on a plate for you.

After washing the breakfast dishes, she immediately put something on the stove for dinner, which was served at noon. The menu varied, but seasoned pinto beans or green bean with new potatoes and steamed okra on top of the beans, yellow squash casserole or fried squash, cream potatoes made with butter and whole milk from our farm, sliced tomatoes, meat (from our farm or Daddy's hunting), and cornbread or biscuits were often cooked by Momma.

In the summertime, before it got too hot, Momma would don a straw hat, long-sleeved shirt, pants, and a pair of old shoes and go early to the garden to pick fresh vegetables. After she picked the fresh vegetables, she would prepare them. It was not unusual to see her sitting under the hickory tree by the wood pile shucking and silking corn from the garden. In the summer as well as in the winter, there was always a variety of vegetables to eat because Momma always canned or froze enough vegetables to last her family through the winter and until the garden started producing vegetables the next year. I never remember getting tired of Momma's cooking, and I still enjoy cooking and eating meals, especially vegetables prepared by our Momma's recipes. Recipes not necessarily written down but passed down to me through the years of watching her "steady pace" in the kitchen.

Living in a childhood home with no running water required a tremendous amount of labor to keep a supply of water in the home. As children, we all helped Momma by drawing water from a well with a well bucket for use in the kitchen and bringing buckets of water from a cedar tank to provide the rest of the household water needs.

Throughout the day, Momma maintained a "steady pace." When Momma snapped green beans, shelled peas, or peeled potatoes, she would sit down to do these tasks. That was her rest period.

Wash day was just that. Using a wringer washing machine or scrub board, Momma washed our clothes, hung the washed clothes on a clothesline in the yard to dry, brought the dried clothes in the house, folded the clothes, and the next day ironed what was wrinkled. She didn't use fabric softener, but I can still remember how fresh the clothes smelled after blowing in the breeze on a sunny day after hanging on a clothesline. When folding the clothes, Momma would smooth out the wrinkles so she didn't have to iron everything, but in that time period even the handkerchiefs were ironed. That was my job.

On rainy days, Momma would often sew; she made most of her clothes and mine. At first, she used a Singer treadle sewing machine. When she got her new electric sewing machine, she placed it on top of the Singer machine cabinet. I would sit at her feet making clothes for my dolls while she sewed our clothes.

Daddy farmed for a living. When Daddy was working his tobacco patches, stripping tobacco, cutting firewood, or gardening, Momma, my brothers, and I helped him. There is no telling how many miles Momma walked operating a gooseneck hoe or how many tomato plants Momma tied up for Daddy because he disliked these tasks.

When suppertime came, we would go to the table and remove the tablecloth that covered the bowls of food left from dinner that were covered with saucers or lids instead of saran wrap. Momma cooked enough food at dinner to have food left for supper. We would eat the leftovers from dinner for supper; I don't remember anyone ever complaining about what we had to eat. We weren't required to clean our plates, but if you took out too much food and didn't eat it, it would be left for you to eat the next meal or next day. I only remember making that mistake once. We didn't waste food at our house because Daddy had seen children starving when he was in the war; he would remind us that we should be thankful we had enough to eat.

If anyone came by our house at mealtime, they were invited to eat the meal "with us at our table." This included hired hands (teenagers and kids Daddy recruited for potato digging, tobacco cutting, and hay hauling), kinfolks, neighbors (Delbert Morgan at least once a week), visiting preachers, and a traveling Bible salesman. Momma never discriminated at her table. As I recall in the 60s, when an African-American teenager was helping my older brother and Daddy haul manure, a woman helping Momma and me with the meal asked Momma where she was going to seat the young man. Momma said, "At the table with the other men. He worked with them; he is going to eat with them." Even though I was only a child, I realized the stand that Momma made that day was profound. Momma always loved and treated everyone equally regardless of the color of their skin, age, or status in life.

After Momma passed during her visitation, two comments were said over and over: "Your mother was a good Christian woman and an excellent cook," and it didn't matter if the person was in their nineties or teens; the comments were the same. In fact, I had to smile when a family friend's teenage son reminisced how rough it was helping Daddy dig potatoes but said, "Your Momma sure cooked a good dinner for us!"

Momma always encouraged us to get an education. After the supper dishes were washed, Momma would help us with our school lessons when we were in grade school. Often Momma would fall asleep as we read from our readers about Alice, Jerry, and Jip (the dog). As a child I wondered why Momma couldn't stay awake while we were reading. Now as an adult, I realized that even a "steady pace" from sunrise to sunset is tiring.

When my younger brother was in high school, Momma went to work as a cook in the dietary department at a nursing home to provide additional income for him to complete school. This meant she had to get up at 4:00 A.M. to get ready, eat, take an insulin shot, and drive to work to cook breakfast for the residents. She later changed jobs and went to work at the school lunch program. She loved cooking for the children, the hours were better, and she was off in the summer so she had more time to tend her garden and can or freeze her garden vegetables. After high school, my younger brother went to electronic school in Kentucky; Momma continued helping him with his school expenses. I remember hearing Daddy say to Momma, "You are wasting your money."

Momma quickly replied, "I can't think of anything else that I would rather be spending my money on."

Momma encouraged me every step of the way as I completed my education and started working as a registered dietitian. After our children were born, I struggled with whether I should continue working or stay home and be a fulltime mother. When I talked to Momma about my dilemma, she wisely said, "You have spent years getting an education; it would be a shame to not use it. You can be a good mother and work as a dietitian." Now I see if you maintain "a steady pace" you can do most anything you set your mind to do, including working a job and maintaining a home.

After work, Momma would stop by her sister's house to check on Ma (her mother) while her sister was still at work. Ma, as well as other shut-ins through the years, enjoyed her visits.

When Momma retired from working with the school lunch program, she continued to maintain a steady pace as long as her health permitted. Even though she was diagnosed with Alzheimer's disease in 2000 by Dr. Roger McKinney, she continued to enjoy snapping green beans, shelling peas, and folding towels. She always seemed happy when she was doing something to help others.

After Momma got sick, Daddy made some changes. He no longer kept a milk cow because Momma wasn't able to milk the family cow, and this was a job he didn't want to do. Also, he bought a small mule and hobbled it around the yard because it was no longer safe for Momma to mow the grass, and he didn't want to mow. Later, he had my older brother mow the grass weekly. Amazingly, Daddy learned to cook breakfast, use the microwave to warm the meals that I cooked weekly for them, give Momma her insulin shots, and operate a broom. All chores he had never done since with Momma's "steady pace," he didn't see the need to do any of these chores before. One day when I was at my parents' home to complete my weekly chores for them, Daddy said, "I never realized what it took for a woman to run a household."

"Yes, I know, Momma made it look easy, but it's not," I said.

The most remarkable change Daddy made after Momma was diagnosed with Alzheimer's disease was he started reading the Bible to her out loud. Even though Daddy had a tenth-grade education and reading was not his best subject, Momma enjoyed Daddy reading the Bible to her. As Daddy read the Bible to her, the Holy Spirit pricked his heart when he read Mark 16:16: "He that believeth and is baptized shall be saved; but he that believeth not shall be damned." Daddy realized even though he had a Christian mother and wife, he had never been obedient to God. He accepted Jesus into his heart and life. He said he had to be baptized in obedience to God and he was on 5/25/2005 with family, including Momma, in attendance.

Our spiritual development was always a priority for Momma. She carried her children to church every time the church doors were open, even though Daddy rarely went with us. During the August revival week, she adjusted her household chores so she could go to morning and evening services. Church attendance was not a duty for her; it was a joy in her life.

Even after her son, David, died as the result of a farming accident, she remained faithful to God. Before his accident, Momma told her husband and her Sunday School class she didn't think she would raise David to be an adult; she felt like something was going to happen to him. As an adult, I realized God had prepared his faithful daughter for the loss of her son. After I had children, I realized even more how painful the loss of David was for her as a mother. When I asked Momma how she was able to bear losing a child, she said, "In the first place, our children belong to God. He just loans them to us for a while. Sometimes He calls them home to be with Him."

Momma always prayed for her husband, children, grandchildren, and the lost (ones who had not accepted Jesus as their Savior). In 2006, after she passed, I found a rough draft of a letter she had written years ago to a pastor who was retiring. In the letter she thanked him for his faithfulness to our church and asked that he continue to pray for her husband and one of her children who had not publicly made a profession of faith because she wanted to be sure that they were saved.

Yes, Momma, your prayers were answered when Daddy was saved and baptized 5/25/2005, after he was convicted by the Holy Spirit as he read the Bible to you due to your Alzheimer's disease. After my brother recovered from Covid-19, I shared with him that I had begged God to spare his life; I had already thanked the Dear Lord that he had. I just wanted to know if he had made his reservation for Heaven if he hadn't survived Covid.

He said yes, he had! "Yes, I agree our Momma maintained a 'steady pace' not only in her work ethic but, most importantly, in her daily walk with the Dear Lord through the years!"

Dearest Momma, thank you for being our example of a virtuous woman. Even though you have been gone for years now, your legacy lives on in our hearts!

References:
Mark 16:16 (KJV)
Proverbs 31:10-31 (KJV)

Our Dear Mrs. Lucile

On the 175th-year celebration of Fall Creek Baptist Church's existence, a homecoming service and potluck dinner were planned. Former pastors and members were invited to participate in the day's events. The oldest living member, Mrs. Lucile, who was in her nineties at the time, was asked to share her memories of Fall Creek. After her remarks, one of the deacons asked her questions to prompt her memory regarding the history of the church. When she was asked, "Who was your favorite pastor during your years of being a member of the church?" she promptly and wisely replied, "The current pastor was always my favorite. I loved and prayed for them all."

Her comments reminded me that through the years after the pulpit committee (AKA search committee) presented a candidate for the pastor position, the church voted by secret ballot. When the votes were counted, the chairman of the deacons would give the secret ballot results. If the candidate received 75% of the vote, the deacon would present the name of our new pastor that the church was calling. Then he asked that the church make it a unanimous decision "in support " of the man God had led us to call as our pastor.

As Mrs. Lucile was exiting the podium steps, one of our deacons raced over to assist her out of respect and fear that she might fall. Mrs. Lucile remarked with a big grin, "You're treating me like I'm an old person," but wisely accepted his arm as she elegantly descended the steps. The congregation was elated, and we burst into a round of applause for our dear Mrs. Lucile.

Reference: "Who can find a virtuous woman? Her price is far above rubies" (Proverbs 31:10, 30, and 31).

Handwritten Notes

While deep cleaning, or rather decluttering my grown daughter's room—a room she hasn't slept in for twenty years—I found among her selected childhood collectibles two handwritten notes. As I glanced at the notes, I immediately recognized Mrs. Mildred's lovely handwriting. Mrs. Mildred, a devoted Sunday School teacher of Fall Creek Church for decades, was known for her notes of encouragement especially written to the youth of our church, and this note was no exception. As her precious words flowed across the paper expressing thanks and appreciation for my daughter using her talents for the Lord, I smiled as I remembered her kind words to me as a child when she prayed with me on more than one occasion. Her closing words, "We have such a wonderful group of young people at Fall Creek. All of you have a special place in my heart. I love all of you. Keep up the good work. May God Bless. Love, Mildred E.," felt like words inspired by the Dear Lord. I don't think Paul's writings to Timothy were any more fitly written.

It has been said, "It takes a village to raise a child," but once again, we are reminded that one person can make an impact on a child's life, and that person will be fondly remembered and treasured by that child forever.

Thank you, Mrs. Mildred E., for leaving us a path to follow by your example as we humbly attempt to inspire future generations in their walk with the Lord."

Reference: "A word fitly spoken is like apples of gold in pictures of silver" (Proverbs 25:11).

Contentment

On a picture-perfect autumn day, my husband and I attended the estate auction of my husband's brother-in-law's parents. As the bids for the sixty-two-acre farm that had been cut into sixteen tracts soared, my sister-in-law sadly commented that her mother-in-law, Mrs. Kathryne, never wanted to buy anything for herself. She was saving her money for her children.

I realized Mrs. Kathryne had been a perfectly content Christian woman living, by today's standards, a simple life. As a farmer's wife, mother, grandmother, and great-grandmother, in reality she had and now has "riches untold" because she is a "child of the King."

So I heard myself say to my sister-in-law, "She would be happy her children will inherit her money; she had everything that she needed and could possibly want."

My husband and I left before the auctioneer sold Mrs. Kathyne's personal property. As we drove away, I commented, "I had planned to buy a small keepsake in remembrance of her, but I don't need any of her possessions. I have already been gifted a treasure from her."

What treasure, you may ask?

"Her example of how she lived her life in the forty-six years that I had the privilege of knowing her. Her legacy of contentment, having an attitude of gratefulness and thankfulness that turned what she had into enough, will live long after she has gone on to her well-deserved Heavenly reward."

Rise and Shine

After days and days of rain, I noticed raindrops starting to fall on my windshield as I drove to work early on a Monday morning in June. *Oh, no,* I thought as my wipers struggled to clear my view.

Since I was a farmer's daughter and a farmer's wife, rain usually doesn't affect my mood since I view rain as a blessing from God bringing much needed moisture to the earth and, in my childhood days, a day of rest from most farm chores, but today I dreaded going to work and dealing with individuals who would be depressed because it was raining.

Usually, as I drove to work, I used the time to meditate, pray, and praise God, but today I was silent as I felt sorry for myself.

As the rain continued to pour down, I was reminded of mornings during my teen years.

When I was a teenager, my days were filled with too many activities—school, extracurricular activities, farm chores, studying daily, and church three times a week. Because I lived in the country, I had an hour-and-fifteen-minute commute plus two bus changes to get to school by 8:00 A.M.; therefore, I had to get up early to get ready to catch the first bus. I never remember missing the bus, but for years after I finished high school I had nightmares that I had overslept and missed the bus, which was totally ridiculous because my mother always woke me up every morning. When she came into my room, she would cheerfully shout, "Rise and shine, time to get up!" As annoying as her wakeup calls were, I never complained to her because I knew she had already been up for over an hour cooking breakfast and doing other morning chores.

As I smiled thinking of my mother's sacrifice and contributions to my life, I started singing aloud, "Arise and shine and give God the glory, glory. Rise and shine and give God the glory, glory. Rise and shine and give God the glory, children of the Lord." I said, "Thank you, Dear Lord, for my precious Momma and for your wakeup call. I feel sooooo good."

Reminder: When we are having difficult days, remember to praise God and we will feel better.

In September 2019, our daughter started a new adventure at the science museum. My only concern was she had to work on Sunday and would not be able to attend church. Knowing that we all need spiritual food to stay strong in our daily walk with the Lord, I started sending her a Sunday morning "Rise and Shine" devotional to her phone.

Snake Handling

On a Saturday, I eagerly phoned my daughter to see how her adventures at the science museum were going. She sounded tired, as she adjusted from working nights to normal daytime hours.

As I clattered away about my inspirations for "Rise and Shine" devotions for people who have to work on Sunday and can't attend church, she listened politely and then said, "That is something you might need to do."

Finally, I said, "What was the most interesting adventure you had this week?"

She said, "Learned how to handle a snake. The snake has been sick, and it's my job to feed and take care of him."

"How did that go?" I asked.

"Well, I have never been phobic about snakes. At first I was nervous, but I had to overcome my fears."

"That is amazing," I said, thinking about my last experience with a snake. My Biblical fear took over, and I took care of the poor thing as the other two women in the room stood on chairs screaming.

On Saturday night my daughter texted me: "I got my card! It's awesome! Thanks so much."

The encouragement card had a dog on top of a high slide looking afraid. The card said: "Anything worth doing can be a little scary at times. You got this. I believe in you." I added, "I enjoy hearing about your adventures at the science museum, Love always, Momma."

Handling our fears with God's help is less traumatic for us and the snake than handling our fears on our own.

Jesus: Nothing Else Will Satisfy Your Soul

As I cleaned out the clutter in my closet, I came across a worn old faded T-shirt that I had saved because it was special to me.

My daughter wore the T-shirt over twenty years ago, when she was a teenager and was active in the high school fellowship of Christian athletes. Years ago, because of the tattered condition of the T-shirt she tossed it in the throwaway pile. As a child of parents who were Depression-Era babies, I retrieved the T-shirt, carried it to the farm cabin in Kentucky, and wore it for years when I was doing chores, but finally the tears in the T-shirt became so large I had to discontinue wearing it because it no longer covered by body modestly.

As I read the familiar words on the T-shirt one more time, "Jesus: Nothing else will satisfy your soul, " I thought. *Timeless words that have remained true through the generations.*

Inspired, I snapped a picture of the Jesus T-shirt and sent the photo to my daughter for a Sunday morning "Rise-and-Shine Devotion."

Climbing Up the Ladder

As I stood on a twelve-foot ladder cleaning out the decaying leaves in our cabin's gutters, my husband stood on the ground below holding my ladder as I carefully tossed the debris to the ground with gloved hands. Three thoughts came to my mind: 1. If the neighbor men drop by for a visit, they will never let my husband live it down that his wife was on the ladder and he was safely on the ground. 2. I've always been afraid of heights, but through the years my fear has lessened. 3. It's amazing how one can conquer their fears if they have someone they trust to hold their ladder.

There's a gospel song, "They're Holding Up the Ladder," that says, "I know my Savior's with me, and He's teaching me to climb. They're holding up the ladder that I'm climbing on."

Through the years, I wondered how many times the Lord has been with me and I didn't realize it. The answer for me is "too numerous to count."

Later, on the phone, I updated my brother about my gutter-cleaning project. I said, "I'm getting older; I think it's time to call a leaf-guard gutter company."

He said, "I thought the same thing last week when I had to clean my gutters out."

"...I'm climbing up the ladder and I'm going home; at the top of the ladder, oh, what joy there will be, and the angels are holding up this ladder for me...."

Walk the Walk

On a Saturday, my husband and I met at the church with three ladies from my Sunday School class to go visit the shut-ins of our church. Before we left the church, I asked my husband to pray for our visits and traveling mercies. Throughout the day, I continued to ask him to pray at each home and ask the blessing for our lunch at the restaurant. At the end of the day, I realized I had heard my Godly husband pray to God eight times. Each prayer was a special blessing as he talked to God—his Heavenly Father—on behalf of the individuals present in the room. I thought, *I never tire of hearing my husband pray. Maybe it's because I never heard my Daddy pray.*

A few weeks ago, I started sending our daughter a "Rise and Shine" devotional on Sunday morning because she was scheduled to work on Sunday and unable to attend her church. After hearing her Daddy pray eight times on Saturday, I decided on Sunday to send her a picture of her Daddy that she had snapped in 1999 as he walked on his beloved farm. Around the picture she had written John 3:16: "For God so loved the world that he gave his only begotten Son that whosoever believeth in him should not perish, but have everlasting life."

I texted: "Dear God, thank you for daddies who point us closer to you by walking the walk and not just talking the talk. Amen. Rise and Shine and give God the glory children of the Lord."

Proverbs 22:6

The pain in the center of my chest felt as if a knife had been stabbed in my heart as I heard my loved one say something. The look in those eyes let me know the news was not good. My pain was not letting up but was getting harder as if someone was twisting the blade of the knife around in my heart. I caught a few words of the conversation—bits and pieces of this morning's events. I knew this was bad.

The remainder of the day I felt numb. I was stunned with disbelief. It had been almost five years without a problem. Why now a relapse?

That night I continued to feel pain in my chest as I crawled into my feather bed and sunk myself into the bed, hoping for relief.

As I prayed to God for comfort, help, and direction on how to help my loved one, my tears started to flow in the darkness of the night. As I cried I felt the pain in my chest lessen like the knife was slowly being removed. I cried for over an hour; I finally said, "God, I've done my best and it's not enough. My loved one is in your hands." I thanked God one more time for His mercy that no one was hurt, killed, and my loved one's life was spared one more time, but I realized God's patience might be wearing thin for my wayward loved one.

As my tears ceased, I felt at peace that God understood and would be with me whatever I had to face, including the possibility of seeing my loved one suffer.

I wondered why I had not seen my loved one was in trouble, but I realized there were signs. Even last night as I read my Bible, I was torn between two verses: Proverbs 22:6 and "Whatsoever you sow you reap." Also, I thought I had smelled alcohol when I was around my loved one, but the personality change of being grouchy and meanspirited about the simplest things should have clued me in. Did my loved one not remember being loved and supported during the good times as well as the bad times?

As I meditated on these thoughts, I was once again reminded of God's promise found in Proverbs 22:6. Clinging to those comforting words, I mercifully drifted off to sleep.

Every Day Is a Choice

After yet another disastrous alcohol-related event, my older brother said to me, "You sure have a lot of people in your life who have trouble with alcohol for someone who doesn't drink."

"Yes, I know," I said softly.

Several years ago, I stopped by a local fellowship house in the afternoon to pick up a schedule of meetings for a loved one. After I entered the small brick building, I realized I had walked into a room of twenty-plus individuals who were in the middle of an AA meeting. Not wanting to disturb the meeting, I quickly sat in the first available chair next to the door. I then realized unlike church, AA meetings fill up from front to back to leave room for the people who arrive late.

As I sat quietly in the meeting, individual after individual, male and female, young and old, rich and poor poured out their hearts and anonymously shared their stories with the group.

After everyone in the group had finished their story, the informal leader looked at me and asked, "What is your story?" Every eye in the room stared at me in anticipation of what I had to say.

I said, "I actually came by to pick up a meeting schedule for a loved one." Then I began my story.

"My experience with alcohol happened when I was in college and came home at Christmas. Every year, Momma made homemade boiled custard. This year since I was eighteen, it was decided I was old enough to have a teaspoon of Jack in my glass of boiled custard" (AKA Jack Daniels whiskey; this group needed no explanation of what Jack I was talking about). "As I drank the boiled custard, I thought this is the best boiled custard Momma has ever made. When I got to the bottom of the eggshell-thin glass with the pattern of a grapevine etched on the outside, I took my spoon and scraped the bottom of the glass to get every drop. It wasn't until I took my tongue and was going around the rim of the glass that the Holy Spirit inside me said, 'Put the glass down, girl, it's not the boiled custard that you are craving; it's the whiskey.' I listened to my inner voice and set the glass down.

"Every year at Christmas, I make a batch of homemade boiled custard. I pour the boiled custard into the eggshell-thin glasses that I inherited from my Momma, but I do not add the whiskey because I know it wasn't the boiled custard that I craved over forty years ago; it was the whiskey.

"Therefore, even though I have attended many functions where alcohol was served, I have remained a teetotaler because I realized at the tender age of eighteen I liked the taste of whiskey. Every day is a choice. I choose not to drink alcohol."

As I finished telling my story, I realized every eye had been fixed on me and every ear had been tuned to my words as I anonymously poured out my heart to this group of strangers, sharing a story of my youth that I had never told before. The room was totally silent.

Finally, the informal leader cleared his throat, thanked me for sharing my story, and said, "Let's get a meeting schedule for your loved one."

I continue to be thankful to God for the Holy Spirit's daily guidance in my life, and I am happy to report my loved one has been sober for years now, but I am reminded, "Every day is a choice. One has to choose not to drink alcohol."

God Gives Us Peace

As my loved one was leaving my home, my loved one shared a future decision. I was gravely concerned and worried about the plan. I expressed that I realized as a grown individual, one has to make decisions about one's life, but I entreated my loved one to pray to God daily on the matter and I would do the same.

After my loved one left, I washed the dishes and finished folding laundry while I pondered the future decision. As I prayed to God for guidance on the plan, I reached for my Bible and *Daily Guidepost 2019 Devotional*. I opened the book, turned the pages to the bookmarker, and realized I was two days behind in reading the daily devotionals as the bookmarker flagged Tuesday. On that day, the writer reminded the reader the Jewish day begins at sundown—with evening first, then morning. So a new day starts at night fresh and clean without a track in it, just like fresh snow on the ground. When we go to bed the day starts. Therefore, we're not to carry our worries and concerns from the day to bed with us. "Thank you, Dear Lord, for that update on my loved one's decision," I prayed and went to bed.

The next morning, I woke up early before sunrise. As I lingered in my bed enjoying the comforts of the warm covers and a well-rested body from a God-given good night's sleep, I reflected on the conversation I had last night when my loved one came by for supper and a visit. I heard a dove cooing peacefully, faintly in the distance. Because our home is so airtight, we rarely hear outside noise; I thought I was dreaming or hallucinating. The dove cooed two more times. I smiled and thanked the Dear Lord for the peace that only He can give when we trust Him with our life's decisions.

In 2017 God inspired me to write "God Gives Us Peace."
(Dedicated to all Christians living in these last days)

Chorus: God gives us Peace. God gives us Peace.
God gives us Peace that can't be taken away.
Verse 1
In these troubling last days so often the news is bad.
Our souls become sad 'cause we lay our Peace down,
Verse 2
In these troubling last days so often our hearts are sad
'cause we let troubled folks steal our Peace away.
Verse 3
At the end of our days, when we are laid down,
God will give us a peaceful home that can't be taken away.

"Thank you, Dear Lord, for your reminder that only You can give us Peace," I prayed.

The Prayer

On day seven of praying to my Heavenly Father to heal our precious loved one, I lay in my bed before sunrise and searched for the words to utter, but none came to my mind. Then the Dear Lord gave me the words to pray:

Anoint the doctors, nurses, and caregivers with Godly wisdom to restore our precious loved one's much-needed health.

Anoint our precious loved one with Godly wisdom to accept the care you send to restore our loved one's health to a new normal.

Anoint our loved one's family with Godly wisdom so we will know how to provide support and encouragement as our loved one copes with this unexpected change in health.

Thank you, Dear Lord, for reminding me my greatest hurts have led to ministries. Therefore, I see, Dear Lord, that you have already given our precious loved one an education in an area of study that when our loved one's health is restored, you may anoint our loved one to minister to others because our loved one has already walked a mile in their moccasins.

Yes, Dear Lord, I realize some would question your plan for our lives, but diabetics make great diabetic educators, recovering alcoholics are effective counselors in rehab programs, individuals who have lost loved ones are compassionate grief counselors, and the list of individuals who you have used to help others goes on and on, but the one most chilling example was given by an elderly woman at our country church. She said, "I never cared about the people at the local jail. When I saw them on the side of the road picking up trash, I thought of them as jailbirds, but after my grandson went to jail...." She stopped and, with tears flooding her eyes, she said, "I see them differently now. I have compassion for them."

Therefore, "Heavenly Father, I pray that you will anoint us all with a fresh dose of Godly wisdom, and if it is your will, may we view our hurts as an opportunity to minister to others who are hurting. In Jesus' name, I humbly pray."

Reference: Romans 8:26-28 (The Living Bible)

Daddy's Watermelons

As I glanced at the little green-striped sugar-baby watermelon resting in the corner of my cool kitchen floor on my worn-out brown 1970s linoleum, my mind drifted back to earlier days.

As a child, one of the highlights of the hot days of summer (pre-AC years) was Daddy's delicious watermelons. Daddy saved the seeds from a large watermelon that Uncle Mac cut at a family reunion. Every year thereafter, he planted his watermelon seeds and saved the best seeds from that year's crop for next year's planting. Through the years, Daddy raised a ton of watermelons that he enjoyed selling. Each year under Daddy's meticulous care, the watermelons got bigger and bigger. In fact, one source of pride for Daddy was one year winning first place at the county fair for his watermelon.

As Daddy got older, he continued growing the same humongous watermelons, but he recruited my brothers to help him pick and load the melons in his old blue truck. Realizing Daddy was older and needed to make a change, I suggested that since most families were smaller now and didn't need a jumbo watermelon, a smaller melon would be easier to handle and store in the refrigerator. So I suggested he change and raise sugar-baby watermelons—same great taste, just smaller. Daddy listened politely, but he never changed his watermelon seeds. He kept growing the same variety of watermelons because that was what he loved and wanted to do. In fact, after he passed I found his saved watermelon seeds in the freezer waiting for next year's planting season. I divided the watermelon seeds into three piles and placed them in three bags. I kept a bag of seeds for myself and gave the other two bags to my brothers. I told them these seeds were our Daddy's watermelon seeds—part of his legacy and our inheritance. My seeds are still in a small blue corked vase. Homer gave his seeds to a friend, who started growing the watermelons and even sent some of the seeds to California to be planted. Charles never said what he did with his watermelon seeds.

So why didn't I plant my inherited watermelon seeds on our farm in Kentucky? I had eaten so many watermelons as a child. I was founded on watermelons. It was years before I had a taste or a desire to eat a watermelon, even though I would stop by the large display of watermelons at the store and thump the melons (like Daddy had taught me) to see which ones were ripe. When thumped with one's finger, the ripe melon will have a hollow sound, but when you get home with the melon don't eat it the first day or two. Instead, place the watermelon in your cool house on the floor for a few days. Next, place the watermelon in the refrigerator and let it chill. Now your watermelon is ready to cut and serve to your family and friends. When they eat the watermelon after following this procedure, they will say that it is the best watermelon that they have ever eaten because the watermelon is actually ripe. So as I finished writing these reflective words, I decided it was time to move my little sugar-baby watermelon to the refrigerator to chill. In my mind, I can almost taste Daddy's sweet, cold summer watermelons of my childhood.

As I thought about Daddy's unwillingness to change his watermelon seeds to little sugar-baby seeds, I wondered how many times God has presented us a need to make a change in our lives and we chose to continue to do what we want to do even though His way would be better for us.

The Christmas Box

On March 7, 2019, I delivered my last Christmas present of 2018 to my brother Charles. Yes, I know that was seventy-two days late, but life's mitigating circumstances had prevented me from giving him his present in person or sending it to him. My tardiness was not due to lack of preparation, as I had purchased three five-pound boxes of block cheese on 12/13/2018 (one for each of my two brothers and one for me) and three boxes of saltine crackers. My tardiness was not due to lack of instructions since Daddy had told me Christmas 2006 to be sure that after he was gone to continue his Christmas tradition of buying a Christmas box of groceries for my brothers and me. He even wanted to give me the last remaining descendent of old Girlie—our family milk cow—to finance our Christmas boxes. After he passed, I had to tell my brother, Homer, I couldn't accept the cow since I thought she was too old to tolerate the trip to Kentucky; also, she was hopping from old-age arthritis and I was concerned someone might get the idea she was sick and quarantine our farm.

Daddy was particular about his Christmas boxes, but one year Daddy left the box of cheese out of each of our Christmas grocery boxes. I asked, "Daddy, did you forget to buy the boxes of cheese this year?"

He replied, "No, the cheese was higher this year since milk has gone up in price, so I didn't buy the cheese." We all missed our cheese that year.

I said, "Daddy, everyone loves cheese. Why not get the boxes of cheese and omit all the other groceries in the boxes? It would make shopping easier." Of course, he had to do it his way, but I noticed we always had cheese in our Christmas boxes after that year.

Over the years, I have modified the Christmas grocery boxes to be five pounds of cheese, crackers, and bounty from our farm. Every year I tease my brothers, "I bought you cheese this year. I just wanted you to know you're still worth a box of cheese. Haha."

After Christmas cooking 2018, I was down to a third of the box of my cheese and I still had Charles' box of cheese in the back of the refrigerator. I went to a store in Lebanon to get cheese; the store shelves were almost bare. I asked one employee, "Why are the shelves almost empty?"

She said, "The store is closing."

I was devastated. "Where am I going to buy my cheese?"

She said, "The store in Gallatin is still open."

The next day I drove to Gallatin and bought three boxes of cheese. Unknowingly, my husband bought a five-pound box of cheese in Lafayette. So now I had twenty-five and a third pounds of cheese in my refrigerator.

On Valentine's Day, I called Charles but we weren't able to arrange a time to meet and get his Christmas box to him.

On March 6th, I called him and said, "This is getting a little ridiculous. I'm off from work tomorrow; I'm bringing your Christmas box to you." We made arrangements for me to meet him in Watertown after he was off work in order to deliver his Christmas box to him.

On March 7th, after I had delivered his Christmas box and started home, I couldn't help but smile and say, "Yes, Daddy, I did what you instructed me to do."

March 4-8th is always a time of remembrance for me, as it is the anniversary of my family saying goodbye to my nine-year-old brother, David, decades ago, but it is also a time of thanksgiving for me since I am thankful for the brothers, family, and friends that are still with me.

Hallelujah

As I left the bank after paying the final payment on a loan that I had for nine years, I felt as though I floated rather than walked to my car as I thanked God for health, strength, and a functioning brain that allowed me to continue to work. I felt total joy in my heart and soul as I expressed my gratitude and praised God. As I started to drive 231 North and head toward the Lebanon square, I sang out joyfully from deep within my soul, "Hallelujah!" Immediately, as in response, three small planes flew by in the sky. Then the third little plane emitted a cloud of smoke. Amazingly, it looked like writing was forming in the cloud of smoke. Peering to read the message through my windshield, I tapped my brakes to slow down in order to have time to read the message in the cloud, but I quickly realized a truck was behind me and I couldn't safely stop and read the message. Even though I had to drive on, in my soul I knew that God had already answered my soul-felt "Hallelujah!"

In a Split Second

As my husband and I relaxed after a busy day by watching rodeo reruns, I was fixated on the clock as the riders attempted to ride rodeo bulls. As the clock counted the seconds: 1, 2, 3, 4, 5, 6, 7, 8, I was amazed at how long eight seconds can be when one is trying to do a next-to-impossible feat, and I was reminded of the reality that a split second can change one's life forever.

We all know what I am talking about. Just before something bad is about to happen, we have a warning that things are about to change. For some, they call it their premonition, others say they feel it in their gut, but for me it is God using the Holy Spirit dwelling in me, directing me in the split-second decisions that I make in my life.

For example, on a Saturday my husband and I were doing chores. As he walked across the porch, he stumbled over a rocking chair footstool that had gotten moved to the middle of the porch instead of being in its usual place under the rocking chair. Even though he staggered after stumbling over the footstool, miraculously he didn't fall. I thanked the Dear Lord he didn't fall and break a hip.

Later in the afternoon, I decided to take some fresh garden veggies to our neighbor. As I was cautiously pulling out of our country driveway after checking both directions, I checked a second time to the right as I was entering the road. I caught a glimpse of a large farm truck coming around the blind curve; I immediately slammed on my brakes, stopped, and backed out of the road as two large farm trucks pulling sprayers zoomed by me. I took a deep breath and thanked the Dear Lord for His protection. I was reminded that in a split second our lives can change forever.

Enjoy the Rest of Your Day

As I dried my hair after a much-needed relaxing swim at the pool, an elderly woman with snow-white hair started talking to me. We exchanged a few words regarding the weather and the usual conversation pleasantries that we reserve for total strangers. As she left the locker room, she cheerfully said, "Enjoy the rest of your day."

My troubled, sad self wanted to say, "No chance I'll enjoy the rest of my day; I'm headed to the funeral home for visitation," but as the woman's peaceful blue eyes seemed to look into my very soul I heard myself say, "Thank you, and you enjoy the rest of your day, too."

Through the remainder of the day, the next week, and the months that followed, as life's difficulties continued to occur, I was reminded of the cheerful now-in-my-mind wise elderly woman's advice: "Enjoy the rest of your day."

Yes, we will all experience problems, hurts, and sadness in our lives because this is earth and not heaven, but we must remember to continue to "enjoy the rest of our days."

Reference: "This is the day which the Lord hath made, we will rejoice and be glad in it" (Psalm 118:24).

Remain Calm

During December 2018's staff meeting, my supervisor conducted a training session on "What to do if you encounter an active shooter." As she discussed the topic, she read an extensive list of suggested actions to take. After every action to defuse the situation, defend oneself, and survive the ordeal was the two-word instruction to "Remain Calm."

As I pondered the simple two-word instruction to "Remain Calm" I realized it was fitting advice for most of life's difficult situations, so I decided to make "Remain Calm" my mantra for 2019.

At the conclusion of 2019, I realized "Remain Calm" proved to be a necessary course of action for most of my days in 2019. "A crazy twist of fate," some might say, but for me "God's provision for my life's journey" in 2019.

The Blanket

In February 2020, as I smoothed out the wrinkles on the cream-colored velvety-soft blanket that perfectly graced our king-size bed in the loft of our Kentucky cabin, I smiled as I remembered the blanket's history.

In 2005, as I was making up my elderly parents' bed in their country farmhouse, I realized their bedding, which consisted of thin, rough sheets, worn-out quilts, and a faded bedspread, needed an upgrade. So I went and made the necessary purchases which included, I thought, the most soothing blanket that I had ever touched. On my next visit, I changed the sheets and replaced several worn-out quilts with the blanket, then I folded and stacked the quilts in a straight chair by Momma's dresser. I said, "You are going to love your new blanket; it's designed to keep you warm without the weight of having a stack of quilts on your bed."

I felt so happy as I left my parents' home that I had replaced their old quilts with a new luxurious blanket.

When I came the next week to complete my weekly chores, I noticed the cream-colored velvety blanket was neatly folded and was stacked in the straight chair. The faded worn-out quilts were back on their bed. I said, "Didn't you like the new blanket that I gave you?"

"It was okay," said Daddy, "but we like our quilts better."

"Okay," I said. The cream-colored velvety-soft blanket remained neatly folded on the straight chair.

After my Daddy died in 2007, I carried the blanket back to my home, put it in my closet, and forgot about the blanket until my husband and I were decorating our loft bedroom in our new cabin in Kentucky.

We purchased a burgundy comforter, cream-colored sheets, and burgundy/cream throw pillows for our matching rocking chairs that faced a large crescent moon-shaped window overlooking our farm. My husband said, "We will need a heavy blanket since the winters in Kentucky are cold."

I said, "I think I already have one that might work." Days later, as we spread the freshly laundered cream-colored velvety-soft blanket on our bed, I said, "This blanket is perfect for our bed." Silently, I said, "Thank you, Daddy and Momma, for your housewarming gift for our new cabin."

Remain Calm... Be Happy

For 2020, I cautiously opted to continue "Remain Calm" as my mantra, but added "Be Happy." Life's journey will always have unexpected challenges and difficulties, so remaining calm will allow one to think and see clearly how God wants one to proceed. Choosing to be happy in the process is what makes our days and, quite frankly, our lives, enjoyable.

During the first few months of 2020, my husband and I attended three funerals: his brother, our sister-in-law's mother, and our brother-in-law's mother. We were still coping with these loved ones passing when the Covid-19 pandemic hit our nation.

"Dear Lord, help me to remain calm, be happy, and remember to enjoy my life as I continue to work in healthcare and shelter in place on my off days during the storm of the Covid-19 pandemic," I prayed.

March 26, 2020, I phoned a friend to see how she was faring during the Covid-19 pandemic. She updated me on her recent stressful days but commented her ninety-nine-year-old mother had instructed her and her husband, "Don't worry." She went on to say, "I don't worry about anything."

My friend said, "Maybe that is how she has lived to be ninety-nine; she's not a worrier."

I said, "She's a woman of faith; she knows God has got this."

"Don't worry; be happy...meaning be content."

In April, my friend called me to say her mother had passed peacefully in her bed just before Easter.

I said, "She went Home for Easter."

Necessity

Since on a Monday I left my lunchbox at work, I was more careful than usual as I packed everything that I thought I could possibly need for my ten-and-a-half-hour Tuesday work shift in healthcare in the midst of the Covid-19 pandemic.

Then it occurred to me to be sure that I was taking the Dear Lord with me since that is the most important necessity to not forget to take with me today and, in fact, every day.

References:

"If God be for us, who can be against us?" (Romans 8:31b (KJV)).

"I can do all things through Christ which strengthenth me" (Phillippians 4:13 (KJV)).

Show Me Your Way

For the second time in six weeks, I poked myself in the eye. "What is wrong with me?" I asked myself.

My inner voice (AKA Holy Spirit) answered, "Get your focus off everything else but what I want you to do. I have been with you through all the days of your life. I will continue to be with you daily. Every other voice, people's comments, and distractions are background noise. Listen only to me, and I will pilot you through life's storms."

"Thank you, Dear Lord," I silently prayed.

In 2018 God laid the words to a song on my heart. The song was about asking God to show me the way daily. The last words of the song, or coda, prayerfully ask, "Just for today; show me Your way."

"Thank you, Dear Lord, for the reminder again that you are my Pilot through life's storms, including the Covid-19 pandemic of 2020."

The Sandwich

After the seventh week of Covid-19 sheltering at home, completing essential work duties within Covid-19 guidelines, and no restaurant food, I was craving a grilled chicken sandwich from a restaurant even though my freezer, refrigerator, and kitchen pantry were stocked with enough food to last for weeks and possibly for the rest of the year if I had to do so.

By 9:00 A.M. at work, I had given my coworker a $5.00 bill. I asked if he didn't mind, would he get me a grilled chicken sandwich with cheese, lettuce, spinach, tomatoes, banana peppers, olives, pickles, and lite mayo when he went to lunch? Thankfully, he agreed to make my purchase and took my money and Post-It note with my sandwich-order specifications.

Later, when he dropped by my office with the requested prized sandwich, I had someone in my office who said, "You didn't ask me if I wanted lunch." He quickly offered to go and get her lunch, but she said, "That's okay; I brought my lunch."

I said, "Actually, I did, too; the sandwich is for supper."

The rest of the day, I looked forward to my grilled chicken sandwich treat. So when 6:00 P.M.—suppertime—finally rolled around, I happily unwrapped my sandwich, added a handful of whole grain chips and a cup of homemade vegetable soup to the meal. Then I topped the meal off with a glass of weak tea—more ice and water than tea. As I peacefully ate my sandwich very slowly, I was truly grateful and thankful for the blessings of my life.

My wise mother-in-law, who was mother to six children, cooked homemade meals for her large family. She once commented to me, "Even a sandwich tastes better if someone else makes it for you."

Dear Mrs. Wrye, no truer words were ever spoken, I thought as I swallowed the last tasty morsel of my grilled chicken sandwich.

The Foolish Cardinal: Part I

Once again for the umpteenth time, I watched a beautiful red cardinal peck and try to fight his own reflection in the large window of our cabin's loft. I said to my husband, "Looks like he would learn his lesson; he just keeps beating his head against the window for nothing."

He said, "He's just trying to protect his turf."

I said, "But he is in no danger; he is just hurting himself. Oh, no." I thought, *How many times have I acted like the foolish cardinal and have been my own worst enemy—sensing danger, problems, and concerns when none existed, instead of letting go of my worries and allowing the Good Lord to fight my real battles?*

The Foolish Cardinal: Part II

As the dreary winter months dragged on, most of the remaining natural vegetation on our farm had turned brown. My husband decided there was not adequate food available for the cardinal who was residing close to our cabin in the woods. So he purchased a bag of cardinal birdseed, which he used to fill an empty birdfeeder that hung on a tree branch near our cabin.

Unexpectedly, the cardinal ignored the birdseed that had been specifically provided for him. After an ice storm and six inches of snow blanketed the ground, my husband decided to move the birdfeeder to the tree branch that the cardinal used for a perch. Several days after the move, my husband commented, "That cardinal has not yet found the birdseed that I provided him."

"How foolish of him!" I replied.

Later, as I looked at the bag of cardinal birdseed, I noted the seeds—sunflower, safflower, grains, and peanut pieces. The bag contained a perfect blend of gourmet birdseed. *How ironic,* I thought. *The cardinal, who is probably physically hungry, has a birdfeeder filled with nourishing seeds, but he is not able to see the seeds; therefore he is not able to enjoy the delicious, nourishing treat provided for him.*

Then the Holy Spirit prickled my soul: "How many times have I provided what you spiritually needed to satisfy your hungering, thirsty soul, and you didn't recognize it either?"

As the words of the old gospel song of my youth flooded my mind, I humbly prayed, "Open my eyes that I may see glimpses of truth Thou has for me. Silently I wait for thee, Ready my God, Thy will to see; Open my eyes illumine me, Spirit divine."

The Foolish Cardinal: Part III

As I looked out the window of our cabin on a cold but sunny day, I noticed a large dark shadow pass over our cabin. *What in the world was that?* I thought as I hurriedly ran outside to investigate.

To my astonishment, I saw a huge hawk descend and land in our garden spot. *Oh, no,* I thought of our foolish cardinal. *I bet that hawk was searching for food.* I was happy I didn't see any red feathers on the ground near where the hawk had landed. "That was a close call for our cardinal."

The close call with the hawk reminded me of the cautionary scripture describing the devil as a roaring lion seeking whom he can devour. Maybe our cardinal was not as foolish as he had appeared to be and "Thank you, Dear Lord, for my reminder to stay on guard since the devil is still on the prowl."

The Lettuce

As I carefully used a small serrated kitchen knife to harvest the tops of my spring lettuce in order to save the root system for future growth, I was reminded of the first spring lettuce that I had seen on a tobacco bed decades ago, when I was a child.

For some reason, we didn't have enough tobacco slips to finish planting one of our tobacco patches that year. So an elderly man in our community, who had finished planting his tobacco patch, offered Daddy the plants that were left on his tobacco bed. On a pleasant, warm, sunny spring day, we went to the man's farm to harvest the much-needed remaining plants from this generous man's tobacco bed. Much-needed, I say, because in that time period tobacco was our family's main cash crop (AKA source of income), and without bumper tobacco crops money at our house would have been slim that year.

We were all totally shocked at how many plants were left on that tobacco bed. It looked like no tobacco slips had been pulled from the bed, but what caught my eye were the numerous perfect lettuce heads mingled throughout the tobacco bed. As I pulled tobacco slips from around the lettuce heads, I commented how pretty the lettuce heads looked and that I had never seen anything like that before, but not one word was spoken by the man or his wife for me to take one of the many heads of lettuce that were left on the tobacco bed. Even though I was a child, I knew better than to ask for a head of lettuce from the couple or to take one.

On the way home, I said to Momma, "I sure would have liked to have had one of those heads of lettuce, but neither one of them offered us a head of lettuce, even though they generously gave us enough tobacco slips to plant a whole patch of tobacco."

Momma said, "They are through with the tobacco plants, but they are still eating lettuce."

I said, "That crisp lettuce would have tasted good on our hamburgers tonight for supper."

Momma said, "It sure would have."

As I closed the lid on a full container of fresh lettuce from my little lettuce bed, I wondered, *Who do I need to share my lettuce with this spring? I'm sure the Good Lord will lay someone on my heart,* and He did.

During one of Joyce Meyer's television shows, she made the comment that "we are truly generous when we give away something that we can use and still want ourselves, not when we give away something we don't need or no longer want."

Candied Sweet Potatoes

Unexpectedly, my husband wagged in a forty-pound box of sweet potatoes and set them on the floor in our cabin. He said, "Wait, I have something else." Then he brought in eight quarts of strawberries. He said, "I went to get strawberries, and the man asked me if I liked sweet potatoes. I said yes, then he gave me a box of sweet potatoes and would not let me pay for them. The man said, 'They are last year's crop; I don't want to sell them, but you can have them.'"

I could hardly wait to cook the sweet potatoes to see if they were any good because last year's sweet potatoes that I bought fell short of our usual expectations. In fact, the last batch I had to boil, mash, cream, and toast a handful of marshmallows on top in order to make them edible.

By 9:00 A.M. the next day, I decided I had waited long enough; I was going to candy some sweet potatoes, one of my father-in-law's favorite foods. Thinking of my dear father-in-law, Pa Wrye, I started the process: Wash the potatoes, slice the sweet potatoes into quarter-inch slices using a cutting board and the sharpest knife in the kitchen. (Remember to use a paper towel under the board to keep it from slipping.) Rinse the sweet potatoes with water. Place the sweet potatoes in a skillet. Add two cups of water. On medium heat, boil the sweet potatoes for five minutes. Drain some of the water, if needed. Add a half-stick of margarine and one and a half cups of sugar. Gently stir until sugar has melted. Cook on medium heat until the sugar, margarine, and water mixture thickens. Turn off the stove. Just before serving the sweet potatoes, warm the candied sweet potatoes. Enjoy.

For dinner, I completed the meal by adding fried chicken, gravy, coleslaw, squash casserole, and a slice of homegrown tomato. The meal, including the sweet potatoes, was delicious. After we finished eating, I said to my husband, "I don't think I've ever served sweet potatoes with this menu before," but like Pa Wrye once said, "Sweet potatoes go with everything!" My husband and I smiled.

Many wonderful meals were shared with my husband's large extended family. Usually the menu included two meats, vegetables, macaroni and cheese, homemade breads, salad, desserts, iced tea, soft drinks, and water, but this particular occasion a summer picnic menu consisting of hamburgers, hotdogs, baked beans, potato salad, chips, corn, homemade ice cream, and cookies was served.

After the meal was consumed, Pa Wrye said to me, "The meal was good, but where were the sweet potatoes?"

Being a registered dietitian who planned menus for healthcare facilities, I said, "Pa, I didn't think sweet potatoes went with this menu."

Pa Wrye said, "Sweet potatoes go with everything!"

"Oh," I said, as I realized Pa Wrye loved sweet potatoes.

So from that day forward, every meal that I cooked for my husband's family or that I attended and brought a dish for the meal, I always brought "candied sweet potatoes."

As Pa Wrye grew older the number of foods that he would eat became less and less, but sweet potatoes always remained one of his favorite foods because "sweet potatoes go with everything."

Children Are a Blessing from the Lord

At 4:00 A.M., I was awakened from a sound sleep by my phone's warning system blaring. As I stumbled down the hallway to retrieve my phone from my purse, I thought, *It's probably a weather advisory,* but to my surprise it was an Amber Alert from the TBI for a child missing in Loratta, Tennessee. I thought, *You have got to be kidding. Where in the world is Loratta, Tennessee?* I went back to bed irritated that I had to be awakened at 4:00 A.M. on my day off from work.

As I drifted back to sleep, fifteen minutes later my phone alarm went off again. I repeated the same actions but thought to myself, *What in the world could I possibly do about this Amber situation that I have to be alerted the second time?* Then one word came to my mind: "Pray." So I said a prayer for the child's safety, turned off my phone, and went back to bed.

At 6:00 A.M., as I was checking my phone, I realized I had received four Amber Alerts for this girl between 4:00 and 4:30 A.M. I said to my husband, "Where in the world is Loratta, Tennessee?"

He said, "It's Loretta, Tennessee; it's in the middle of West Tennessee."

I was still halfway irritated that I had to be bothered with four Amber Alerts before sunrise, in a location I had never heard of before, and there was nothing that I could do but say a prayer for the child. Then the Holy Spirit pricked me: "If that had been your daughter taken from your home in the middle of the night, wouldn't you have wanted the whole state and even the whole nation awake praying for her and trying to locate her in order to return her safely back to you?"

"Yes, yes, Dear Lord!" I said as I prayed for the child's safe return and thanked him for the valuable lesson I had just learned.

At 5:15 P.M., my husband said, "They found that girl that they were looking for this morning."

"How do you know?" I said.

"They just scrolled the update across the bottom of the TV screen," he said.

"Thank you, Dear Lord, the girl is safe," I said to my husband. Then I silently prayed, *"Thank you, Dear Lord, for the reminder that all children are a blessing from the Lord; therefore, we should have love and concern for all children and not just our own."*

Reference: Mark 10:13-16: Jesus blessing the children.

Watching Where I Step

On a crisp fall Sunday morning, I hurriedly closed the electric fence gate to keep the cows and baby calves out of our country yard, garden, and off the porch of our cabin in the woods. As I turned to walk toward the truck, where my husband was waiting for me to join him for our five-minute drive to church, I looked down briefly because something caught my eye.

There was a humongous fresh cow pile that I was about to step in with my Sunday shoes. *Oh, no,* I thought as I quickly adjusted my step to miss the stinky pile.

I breathed a sigh of relief as I opened the truck door and climbed in beside my husband. As he drove us to church, I thought, *I wonder how many times in my life the Holy Spirit has redirected my steps and prevented me from stepping into a disastrous situation?*

"Too many times to count," the Holy Spirit replied within my soul.

Walking in Jesus' Footsteps

As I hummed the gospel song "Footsteps of Jesus," I was reminded that I had always dreamed of traveling to the Holy Lands to physically retrace the footsteps Jesus may have walked in, but due to the Covid-19 pandemic and other concerns I realized travel to a foreign land was not safe or possible now.

In my soul I thought, *Maybe the Holy Spirit is redirecting me to walk in the footsteps of Jesus by humbly serving where he has already led me.*

12/28/2020

Today I feel if I had been born in the animal kingdom, I would be a cross between a mule and a racehorse, even though I know that is not biologically possible since a mule is a hybrid, but on my job I'm working as hard as a mule and as fast as a racehorse.

My Daddy, who was the son of a notable Tennessee walking horse breeder and grandson of a mule trader, always said, "It's in the bloodline; if the filly will trot, so will her colt."

According to Jim Hardy of *Tales of Wells Fargo* fame, "a thoroughbred doesn't stop running when he is still in the race," but I have come to realize there comes a time when even a thoroughbred has to be put out to pasture before he or she drops dead in their tracks.

No One Can Ever Fill Your Shoes

The last two days that I worked before retirement, I had the daunting task of completing my end-of-the-month job responsibilities for the final time around a holiday schedule and training my replacement, who had three months' experience.

Even though those last two days are a blur now, the outpouring of kindness from my friends (AKA coworkers) was memorable. One especially touching moment for me was when one nursing tech presented me with a keychain that had a heart engraved with the words "Enjoy retirement" and "No one can ever fill your shoes."

As I fought back the tears, I said, "Thank you" and "No one can ever fill your shoes either; you are a wife, mother, and grandmother to your awesome twin granddaughters. I remember when you learned you were going to be a grandmother. What a joy they have been in your life!"

She agreed.

Exiting the Building

On 12/30/2020, before I left my office for the final time, I removed five work keys from my old keychain and placed my personal keys on my new retirement keychain that had been gifted to me by a friend. I noticed the weight of my keys was noticeably lighter now; I felt as if a tremendous burden had been lifted from me as I locked my door for the final time and exited the building. I walked across the parking lot and got into my car.

In the darkness, I sat in my car for a few minutes and took several deep breaths to take in this moment of my life. I noticed the cleaning man, our kind friend, leave the building and go to his vehicle. Everyone else had left the building earlier. Time to go home.

As I drove away from my job for the final time, I thanked God for health, strength, and a functioning brain that allowed me to work until retirement. In my heart I knew God had closed this door for me, but through the Holy Spirit's guidance He had already cracked open the next door for me to walk through as I continue to humbly follow in His footsteps.

The First Day of Retirement

On 12/31/2020 (AKA my first day of retirement), I drove fifty miles to our farm in Kentucky. As I turned off Akersville Road and started the eighth-of-a-mile drive to our little cabin in the woods, I noticed the rain and fog had refreshed our pasture and the picturesque view of our Kentucky haven was refreshing my weariness.

"Thank you, Dear Lord; I made it to retirement with you as my Pilot," I prayed.

Fifty years ago, my mother's favorite song was "Jesus Savior Pilot Me," and "Yes, Daddy, you were right; like my Momma I am humbly trying to trot along in Jesus' footsteps."

Each day my retirement chain continues to serve as a reminder to me that no one can ever fill someone else's shoes; we each have to fill the shoes the Good Lord gives us as we humbly walk in his footsteps.

Three Goodbyes

At the end of January, the shadow of sadness still hung over me as I said goodbye this month to three precious souls in my life.

Anita, my first cousin, was three years older than me. As a five-year-old child, I distinctly remember after my brother's horrible accident on our family farm in Norene, Tennessee, being carried to her parents' home in Nashville and being tucked in at the foot of her bed. The comforting touch of her little feet against mine helped calm a child who had witnessed the agonizing events that followed my brother's accident. Even though as adults our paths crossed only occasionally, at rare family events and family funerals, I will always cherish our brief time together.

Teresa, my college roommate during my sophomore year at MTSU, was a blessing from God. Being a college student in the 70s was a challenge complicated by the fact that a great number of young women of that day seemed to go to college to get away from home, party, or obtain their Mrs. degree. Their plan was to find a husband who would support them so they didn't have to work, but Teresa and I both wanted an education. As young women, we realized that to achieve our goal we had to study, attend all classes, get enough sleep, keep our grade point average high, and stay decent (AKA don't do anything to disgrace our family name). It was much easier to stay on track having a roommate who was walking the walk even when no one from home was watching. Even though as adults our paths only crossed occasionally and I didn't learn of her passing until I read MTSU's Winter 2021 magazine, I will always cherish our brief time together.

Joyce, my church friend that I met when we moved to Kentucky, was a special blessing in my life. As I continued to work and prepare for retirement, she was always an encourager to me. Her sweet spirit, positive attitude even as her own health declined, and kindness will always be remembered. Even though our paths crossed too briefly, I will always cherish our brief time together.

"Dear Lord, thank you for the precious souls that you placed in my life as I journey here on earth." Yes, it is goodbye for now, but by faith and according to your word, "I will see y'all again."

Reference: "Then he turned my sorrow into joy! He took away my clothes of mourning and clothed me with joy so that I might sing glad praises to the Lord..." (Psalm 30: 11-12A (TLB)

Skunks

On a sunny January day, my pleasant drive to our farm in Kentucky was disrupted by the stinky aroma of skunks. One of the skunks' remains was left on the side of the road; the remains of the other two were nowhere to be seen, but their distinct stinky smell continued to permeate the air.

As a child, I hated to go to the barn because of the stink, and I don't mean the smell of manure from the farm animals. No, it was the smell of skunk even though there was no skunk anywhere around the barn.

Daddy, who loved trapping, caught a skunk in one of his traps; he decided to remove the skunk's odor sack and place it in the barn. When we opened the door to go to the corn crib or climb the steps to the loft, the smell of skunk would almost overwhelm us. I asked Momma, "What is the reason for the skunk smell in the barn?"

"Daddy's using the skunk odor to open up his sinuses" was the answer I was given.

Don't they make Vicks salve for that purpose? I thought, but never spoke because Daddy was head of his house and what he wanted to do was what was done.

After Daddy passed in 2007, my brothers and I had the overwhelming task of sorting through years of accumulated possessions. During this process, on one occasion I went to the barn. As I opened the latch to the barn door, the now faint but still distinctly stinky smell of skunk filled the air.

As I pondered that a skunk's stinky smell lingers long after he is gone, the Holy Spirit pricked my soul: "We all leave our own distinct legacy after we are gone. Let's pray that it is not a stinky one."

Reference: "We all have happy memories of good men gone to their reward, but the names of wicked men stink after them" (Proverbs 10:7 (TLB).

Cedar Forest: Memories and Lessons Learned

As I read the article "The Splashes Go Silent" in the local newspaper about the swimming pool at Cedars of Lebanon State Park (AKA Cedar Forest by the locals) closing and being possibly changed to a splash pad due to financial issues, I felt a wave of sadness come over me.

Many happy Sunday summer afternoons of my childhood were spent at the original pool with my cousins and friends as my Momma watched over me from a shade tree outside the high chain-linked fence. As a child, I never gave it much thought as to why Momma didn't come inside the fence to the pool area with me, but as an adult I suspect it was the admission fee. Since Momma wasn't going to swim, why pay for something you weren't going to use or didn't need?

In 1971, when the original pool closed, Momma and I moved to the new Olympic-sized L-shaped pool. Even though I was a teenager, Momma continued her supervision of me from outside the fence, but now she was in the sun without a shade tree. Since Daddy was working at the park, the employees decided it was okay for her to move to the refreshment area overlooking the pool and sit under an umbrella, where she could continue to watch over me.

Yes, in the summertime Sunday was church in the morning, swimming in the afternoon, and church at night; the other six days were filled with chores on our family's farm.

As a teenager, one humiliating day for me occurred as we went to one of the farms Daddy was renting. My family was all packed in Daddy's old black truck, a mule had been loaded in the back of the truck, and a plow was tied to the side of the truck bed. On the way to the farm, we met a carload of my friends on Cedar Forest Road. Momma said, "I bet they are going to the pool."

I said, "I know they are because they asked me to go." Since I knew I had to help my family work in the tobacco patch, there was no need to ask permission to go to the pool with my friends.

When we arrived at the tobacco patch, the entire patch was covered in weeds due to an extended rainy period. Daddy started plowing the rows with the mule. Momma, Homer, and I took gooseneck hoes and chopped the weeds that Daddy wasn't able to get with the plow. It took us the remainder of the day to complete the task, but that was how it was done in that time period. Today, the field would probably be plowed, removing the weeds and tobacco plants and new plants planted, but in those days we didn't have extra plants to replant and there was no extra money to purchase more plants.

As an adult, I enjoy swimming year-round at a local family fitness center for exercise. So often people act like exercise is a four-letter word, but I actually view swimming as a pleasure. I can't help but to feel it is because I wasn't able to swim every time I wanted to as a child since I worked with my family to help support us. Also, when I'm swimming my laps, I feel God and Momma's sweet spirit watching over me just like she watched over me swimming at Cedar Forest decades ago.

Lessons I've Learned

#1. Often life can become overwhelming with tasks and responsibilities. In fact, I have observed many coworkers shut down and can't start functioning on the job until they have cleaned and organized their entire desk. My supervisor and I discussed this observation on more than one occasion. My response is a reflection of the tobacco patch that was covered in weeds; we didn't start over, we selected a row and began removing the weeds. Thus, the same approach is needed with overwhelming tasks. Pick a spot and start working. At the end of the day, you will be amazed at your progress. "Thank you, Daddy and Momma, for teaching me how to handle overwhelming situations."

#2. Our children need our supervision as they grow, but sometimes the most effective supervision may be from afar. "Thank you, Momma, for your watch care through the years—with or without a shade tree."

#3. Our children need to learn how to work by doing. Daddy always said, "Don't give a child everything he or she wants even if you can. Don't spoil your children because spoiled children so often become lazy adults."

"Thank you, Daddy, for teaching your children how to work and not spoiling us."

#4. Even though it is often difficult, accept change. Momma missed her shade tree, but she was provided an umbrella in the refreshment area inside the fence. A future generation may enjoy a splash pad and make their own precious childhood memories.

"Thank you, Momma, for teaching me not to complain about change when it's necessary."

#5. Spend your hard-earned money wisely. Don't waste your money on something you can do without and don't even need. "Thank you, Daddy and Momma, for walking the walk and not just talking the talk when managing your money and teaching your children how to manage our money."

The Christmas Peppermint Candy Stick

Early in the morning on the last Sunday of March, as I was searching through my kitchen pantry, I found a giant peppermint candy stick. As I studied the red-and-white peppermint candy stick, I noticed the red stripes were no longer defined; they had blurred with the passing of time. *Oh, I remember when I bought this candy stick,* I thought.

A few weeks before Christmas in 2006, I decided to make a quick stop at a local store to purchase a few items that I needed. As I was checking out some Christmas trinkets at the back of the store, I heard a daughter talking rather sharply to her elderly mother about the Christmas shopping the mother planned to do. The daughter impatiently said, "Mother, I know you want to buy all your grandchildren something, but we don't have much time to shop today."

The elderly mother, whom I now knew was a grandmother, said, "I know, but I would like to get them all something for Christmas. I know I don't have much money to spend, there are several to buy for, and they have everything that they could possibly want, but I want them to have something from me at Christmas."

Overhearing the mother and daughter's conversation, I realized I was missing my own mother, who had passed. Thinking of our happy days of sharing time together, I walked closer to them.

As I looked at some Christmas items near the elderly woman, she picked up a giant peppermint candy stick and excitedly exclaimed, "I can get them all peppermint candy sticks this year! I know it's not much, but it will be something from me."

Then I said to the elderly woman, "Did you get peppermint candy in your Christmas stocking when you were a child?"

The elderly grandmother smiled and replied, "Yes! I did!"

I went on to say, "My mother, who has passed, told me about how Christmas was when she was a child. Times were hard. Our country was in the middle of a depression, but at Christmas each child found peppermint candy, an orange, apple, banana, and some nuts in their stockings on Christmas morning. We were so happy to receive the gifts that had been placed in our Christmas stockings that were actually our own socks that we had hung on the mantel by a real fireplace. We decorated a cedar tree cut from our farm with popcorn strings that we made from corn that we popped and ornaments that we handmade. Ma would cook a big delicious Christmas Day dinner on a wood stove; we had country ham and biscuits, hen, dressing, creamed potatoes, corn, green beans that Ma had canned, dressed eggs, real butter, and cakes that Ma baked. Most of the food on our table was raised on our family farm. The Christmas story from the Bible was read at our home on Christmas Day. We felt so happy, blessed, and loved. So when you give your grandchildren your peppermint candy sticks this Christmas, please remember to tell them your story about Christmas at your home when you were a little girl. You will be sharing your precious memories with them that are truly priceless. Even though my mother is gone now I think about her every day, but I am comforted reflecting on the stories that she shared with me and the memories we made together."

As I finished talking, the elderly woman smiled and, with a twinkle in her eyes, she thanked me for sharing my mother's Christmas story and promised to share her Christmas memories with her grandchildren.

When the elderly mother joyfully went to pay for the peppermint candy sticks, I said to her daughter, "Treasure your mother while you have her because our time with our loved ones is always shorter than we think."

With tears in her eyes, the daughter said, "Thank you."

After they left the store, I finished my shopping trip by purchasing a giant peppermint candy stick too—in remembrance of my Momma.

The Greeter

Years ago, when our friend Bobby passed after a long illness, we all felt a profound void in our lives. The day of his funeral, I was scheduled to work and didn't know if I would be able to leave work to attend a funeral for someone who was not a relative; therefore, my husband planned to go to the funeral without me. Miraculously, the workload was light that day, and I was able to leave work early and make the drive from the hospital to Fall Creek Baptist Church in Norene, Tennessee, with only seconds to spare. As the usher seated me in the last remaining folding chair that had been set up in a Sunday School room for the overflow crowd, the celebration service of a life well lived began. *What a wonderful, uplifting funeral—a reflection of the joy Bobby brought to our lives,* I thought as I exited the church.

In the churchyard, I spotted my husband. As we updated each other on our day's events, we decided that I would pick up our kids at school, he would go home to start his evening farm chores, and we would not attend Bobby's burial at Fairview Cemetery.

Since I didn't go to Bobby's burial, I had this nagging lack of closure in my heart. A few weeks later, when I was at the cemetery putting flowers on my family's graves, I decided to stop at Bobby's grave and pay my respects, hoping this would give me the closure that I needed.

Not knowing where his grave was located, I wandered over the entire cemetery trying to locate his grave. The gravediggers had done such a good job of replacing the sod on the new grave that I couldn't tell where his grave was located. Finally in desperation, I decided to give up and leave the cemetery. As I went to exit the front gate of the cemetery, I stopped in my tracks. There was

Bobby's tombstone—the first one inside the gate. I smiled. "Just like a store greeter, Bobby is greeting us when we enter the cemetery."

Sometime later, when I was sharing my cemetery visit with one of Bobby's numerous friends, I said, "I can almost see Bobby, who loved to talk, loved everybody, and never met a stranger, being a greeter at Heaven's gate. I can almost hear Bobby say, 'Welcome, I've been waiting for you. What took you so long!'" We both laughed.

Years later—July 2019—when one of Bobby's friends died unexpectedly, it was a comfort knowing he would be greeted by Bobby as he entered the Pearly Gates.

In healthcare, when we had patients die, it was difficult for the staff because we became close to our patients due to seeing them three times a week for years. So often we spent more time with our patients than our family members; thus our patients became a part of our dialysis family. When coworkers, other patients, and a patient's family mourned the loss of a passing individual and needed comforting words, I shared my journey.

When I was five years old, my nine-year-old brother died as a result of a farming accident. My mother explained, "Life is a journey—not the final destination. God calls us Home at different stages of life as he makes His Heavenly bouquet. Sometimes He calls a child—in the bud of life, sometimes He calls someone when they are middle age—full bloom of life, and other times He calls the aged—when their petals are falling off."

Through the years, I have had a great number of individuals I've dearly loved die. It is very difficult and sad to bury the people that we love, but by faith I know that I will see them again. I believe that when my life on earth has ended and I cross to the other side, my passing will be easier because I have a multitude of loved ones who have gone on before me to greet me. I can almost hear them saying as I enter the Pearly Gates, "Welcome, I've been waiting for you. What took you so long?"

Glorify God

On Saturday, February 27, 2021, the writer of the devotional encouraged the reader to take a blank sheet of paper and allow the Holy Spirit to inspire and write a vision of oneself on the blank sheet of paper. Immediately, the words were revealed to me—writer: glorify God.

Surprisingly, the words did not seem foreign to me. While sheltering at home during the Covid-19 pandemic, I was inspired by a Christmas service presented by Rolling Hills Church. I selected "Glorify God " daily as my mantra for 2021 and have continued to "occasionally" record stores in my Stellar Notebook when I felt inspired to do so.

While watching a *Jeopardy!* rerun, Alex Trebec read the following question: "What female writer, now seventy years old, at times reportedly wrote twenty to twenty-two hours a day using an old manual typewriter?" After the question was missed by all three contestants, Alex Trebec revealed the correct answer as the famous award-winning novelist Danielle Steele.

How amazing, I thought, but what pricked my soul was *"Surely, you can carve out an hour a day to record your inspired stories to glorify God daily for the remaining days of your life. Yes, it is acceptable to write with pen and paper a rough draft, then a second draft in your Stellar Spiral Notebook, and use an old electric typewriter rather than a computer to type the final version of your stories."*

References: "Invest every day that you have to glorify God" (Rolling Hill Church's Christmas show, 12/25/2020).

"Look for Christ and you will find Him. And with Him, everything else" (C. S. Lewis).

Update: Christmas 2022, my daughter gifted me a Surface tablet to assist me in recording my stories.

But First, PRAY

Last year as our friend Joe so openly shared his testimony and struggles with the small congregation in attendance at church one Sunday, he asked for prayer regarding a decision he needed to make about his employment.

Unfortunately, due to the raging Covid-19 pandemic, we had to cancel in-person church for a period of time. The pastor used Facetime and phone calls to continue to deliver the weekly message. My husband and I tried to stay in touch with our church friends via phone calls and cards. On one occasion, we were updated Joe had changed jobs—less stress, but less money. We both realized this would be an adjustment for Joe and his wife, so we added them to our prayer list.

The third Sunday in February, our church resumed in-person service; no Joe was in attendance. His wife updated that Joe had changed jobs again and was having to work today. On the way home, I said to my husband, "We need to continue to pray for Joe since I'm concerned about his having to miss church. We all know how hard it is to stay on track when we miss the spiritual food that we need."

The fourth Sunday in February, Joe was back in church. After service my husband and I were talking to Joe. He said his new job was going well, great hours, and closer to home. His boss had brought him into the office and said, "We're not paying you enough money for the job you are doing," and gave him a raise.

I said, "Joe, that is unbelievable in today's workplace, where so often companies are trying to pay their workers as little as they can in order to make more money for the company and themselves."

He said, "I know. They are a good company to work for."

Driving home, my heart was pricked: *"You have been praying for Joe's employment situation. Why are you so surprised that your prayers were answered?"*

"Thank you, Dear Lord, for answered prayers," I prayed.

Over the years, I have accumulated a collage of Post-It notes on my refrigerator to inspire and guide me on my daily walk with the Lord. During the employment years, one note, "Do the best that you can and let God take care of the rest," was always an inspiration to me at 4 o'clock in the morning, but on 2/28/21 the Holy Spirit provided me a much-needed update: "But first PRAY, then do your best, and let God take care of the rest."

Barn Troubles

After a storm, my husband called to give me an update from Kentucky. He stated a family in our community lost their hay barn when the wind came through a few nights ago, but remarkably the young family, their recently built home, and their shop were unharmed. I quickly replied, "I'm so thankful they are all safe; they can rebuild the hay barn, but you can't replace a loved one."

Decades ago, when we were newlyweds, my husband and I decided to raise cattle. He purchased a bull and two heifers. We were so excited and enjoyed our small farming operation. Unfortunately, one heifer lost her first calf. We were devastated over our loss. After a church service my husband was sharing our recent farming woes with an elderly family friend. He kindly and wisely stated, "I'm sorry for your loss, but the old-timers always told me if your troubles stay at your barn and don't move to your home you're doing okay."

References: "And we know that all things work together for good to them that love God, to them who are called according to his purpose" (Romans 8:28).

"What shall we then say to these things? If God be for us, who can be against us?" (Romans 8:31).

A Smile...

Once a patient remarked that his grandmother told him years ago, "A smile will carry you a long way." He went on to say, "After my mother died when I was a baby, I went to live with my grandmother; she died. Then I went to live with an aunt; there were a lot of children in the household. There wasn't enough money to go around, so I went to work for a businessman doing odd jobs. When I started high school, I didn't have the clothes I needed to wear to school so the businessman bought my clothes; I was so thankful that I was able to continue my education. Later, I married, and we had children. I have been so blessed in my life; we still meet together as a family for Sunday dinner after church and take vacations together."

The staff and I noted that even though the man was dealing with his own health issues, he was an inspiration to us all.

In 2016, scientists discovered that when you smile even if you don't feel like smiling, it changes the chemicals in your brain and you will feel better. In summary, one recipe to feel better: Smile more. I decided to use the wise grandmother's words and the scientific discovery as a patient educational handout.

In 2020, during the Covid-19 pandemic, we were all wearing masks. As a result, we weren't smiling and we were all feeling the side-effects of smiling less. Therefore, I used the still "timely words" to construct a bulletin board for the lobby as a reminder to smile more.

Thank you, dear one, for your words of wisdom; your inspiring legacy lives on long after you have passed.

Listen to God... You Will Feel Better

As I was sorting through my hodgepodge of cards, notes, and other stationery, I found a pack of "Signs of God" stickers. One red sticker, shaped like a stop sign with the words "Stop, look, and listen to God," caught my attention.

Years ago, I served on a committee at church. There was a difference of opinion among the committee members and some members of the church as to how to proceed. As I pondered on the situation, I started my weekly drive through the state park to my parents' country home to assist my Momma with her chores, as she was in the early stages of Alzheimer's disease. During my drive, the Holy Spirit spoke to me (not verbally, but to my soul): "Jesus didn't have a wife. Most of the disciples and Paul didn't have a wife. The young preacher the committee is considering has a wife, but she can't come with him because she is ministering at the church that they are attending."

When I arrived at my parents' home, my Momma took one look at me and asked, "What is wrong with you?"

I told her what the Holy Spirit had revealed to me during my drive through the park and that I, as well as some of the church members, had felt that we could not recommend the young preacher to the church for a vote unless his wife came with him, but now the Holy Spirit had shown me that I was wrong.

Momma said, "Listen to God, not the people," and I did.

Just as the stop sign prevents disasters on the road, the practice of taking the time to stop, look, and listen to God on life's highway will prevent disastrous results; thus listen to God...you will feel better.

A Perfect Day

As I dragged an almost too-heavy bag of trash from the house to my car, I felt the sun's warm rays soothe my aching body. After I lifted the bag of trash into the trunk of my car and closed the trunk, I lingered longer than necessary to savor the warmth of the day, which was a noticeable contrast to the recent bitter-cold days. Driving to the trash dump, I couldn't help but notice that every yard had a fresh crop of green onions and not a cloud could be seen in the clear blue sky. Leaving the dump, I decided to take the long way home rather than going back the way I came. It was as if I wanted to drink in the beauty of the day and make it last a little longer. As I parked my car in our driveway, I decided to check on the buttercups in the fence row. (Actually, I realize buttercups are daffodils, but Momma always called them buttercups when I was a child, so it seems natural to continue to call them buttercups.) My husband had picked me some for Valentine's Day—a tradition he had done for years. I just wanted to see how the buttercups were faring after the ice and six inches of snow had melted. To my delight, the buttercups were in full bloom. I picked two blooms and some greenery. Happily, I carried my flowers home, found a small vase in the utility room, poured fresh water in the vase, and placed the buttercups in the vase. I set the arrangement on my kitchen table and snapped a picture with my phone of my bouquet to capture the beauty of the day.

"Perfect," I said to myself.

Instinctively, I sat down at my piano, played, and sang "Heavenly Sunlight," a song from my childhood: "Walking in sunlight, all of my journey. Over the mountains, Thro the deep vale; Jesus has said. I never forsake thee. Promise divine that never can fail. Heavenly sunlight, Heavenly sunlight, flooding my soul with glory divine; Hallelujah, I am rejoicing. Singing his praises, Jesus is mine."

"Thank you, Dear Lord, for another perfect day," I prayed. "This is the day the Lord hath made, we will rejoice and be glad in it" (Psalm 118:24).

Repairs

After church one Sunday, a group of members went outside to check out the church sign since during the business meeting it was discussed that the sign was broken; it needed to be repaired or replaced.

As the informal committee surveyed the damage to the sign, we noted the glass was broken on one side. My husband commented, "We can get someone to replace the glass."

The pastor noted the frame was slightly bent; I said, "Someone probably hit it; it's a solid metal frame that could be straightened."

Adam said, "The lightbulb needs to be replaced in order to illuminate the words at night."

Laura suggested some flowers could be planted around the base.

Toni pointed out we already had letters for the sign that were stored in the basement. She also told the pastor where the key to the sign was located. Someone commented that the marker board that had been placed over the original sign slots for the letters could be removed if we decided to use the lettering again.

Finally, our member Adam said, "If we spend a little time, care, and attention to our sign, it can be repaired."

Then I said, "Wise words, Adam. Spending a little time, care, and attention will repair most of life's problems."

"Thank you, Dear Lord, for the reminder that your Sweet Spirit is guiding us as we make a needed church repair and possibly a much-needed repair in our lives."

Survivor of the Covid-19

On the one-year anniversary of the Covid-19 pandemic, a reporter covered the devastation of the pandemic. After the dismal statistics were given, he started interviewing the survivors of the pandemic. One young woman in her twenties, who had been in foster care most of her life, was discharged from the program when she turned eighteen. Before the pandemic, she had a job in a fast-food restaurant and had been able to save three paychecks. Then the pandemic hit. Eight months pregnant, she lived in a tent and went to a shelter to shower and change her work clothes, but due to the capacity limits of the pandemic the shelter was often filled, and she was unable to go to the shelter to shower and change her clothes. Due to the pandemic, the restaurant where she worked closed; she lost her job. Fortunately, she delivered a healthy baby boy and was provided housing by a charity organization. She stated she was thankful for the help she had received, for having a healthy baby, and having a place to live provided for them. She stated she wanted to provide a good life for her baby.

As I contemplated this individual's life story, I was reminded that an attitude of gratitude and thankfulness turn what we have into enough.

"Thank you, Dear Lord, for the blessings you have given me in my life. Please help me to remember to seek your guidance when life's difficulties come my way."

The Harvest Is Plenty and the Laborers Are Few

In 2006, after Momma passed, some spiritual events occurred that I can't explain.

As I sat in my chair reading the Bible in the quietness of the night, I was drawn to the scripture in Matthew that the "Harvest is plenty and the laborers are few." As I read the familiar verses, I wrote on a notepad:

1. Pray laborers will be sent.

2. Be willing to be a laborer when called.

3. If you are unwilling to pray or be a laborer, get out of the way of the ones doing the Lord's work. Don't be a hindrance to the work of the Lord.

I took an ink pen and circled the section of scripture to highlight the urgency of this scripture and the reality that time is shorter than we think.

The next day I asked my childhood friend and her husband, who was a deacon at the church I attended, to take my Bible and notes to give to my pastor since my husband had decided to take me to our farm in Kentucky to see the progress on our cabin that he was building. On Sunday we were going to attend the church in Akersville, which was down the road from our farm.

On Sunday, as we sat in the back row of the small church, the pastor opened his Bible and announced the message for the day: "The Harvest is plenty and the laborers are few," he preached from Matthew 9:36-38. When we got in the truck after the service, I said, "The preacher preached on the same scripture that I sent to our pastor."

My husband said, "I know."

The next Sunday we returned to our home church. I told my pastor, "You're not going to believe this, but the preacher at the church we visited last Sunday preached on Matthew 9:36-38, 'The Harvest is plenty and the laborers are few,' the same words that I was inspired to send you in my Bible."

He said, "Ina, when I stood in the pulpit last Sunday and opened the Bible, I realized I had picked up your Bible instead of mine. I had prepared another sermon but realized the Holy Spirit was directing me to preach 'The Harvest is plenty and the laborers are few.' I used your marked Bible and notes to preach the sermon."

I was stunned, but I really shouldn't have been. By faith, I believe the Holy Spirit moves in mysterious ways, but I hadn't expected him to use me.

Sweet Hour of Prayer

For the opening assembly at church, I played "Sweet Hour of Prayer" on the piano since our Sunday School lesson was on being committed to prayer. After I finished playing the inspiring song, I said, "The title of the song that I played is 'Sweet Hour of Prayer,' not 'Sweet Minute of Prayer.' We have to spend time in prayer with God if we want to have His presence and guidance in our lives."

Times Have Changed but God Hasn't

As I read the wedding invitation for a young couple that was posted on the church bulletin board, I noted the date, time, location, and reception with dinner and dance to follow.

Fifty years ago, I was asked to go to my high school junior banquet/dance by my boyfriend. When I asked permission from Momma to go to the event, she had to think about whether she should let me go to the banquet/dance or not. As I pleaded my case, I listed all the reasons it would be okay for me to go. She listened and said, "I know times have changed, but years ago your great uncle was kicked out of the church for square dancing. He was literally voted out of the church by the then-members. He never went back to church again as far as I remember."

"Oh, how sad," I said.

I was happy when Momma finally decided to allow me to go to the banquet/dance, but due to her hesitation I remembered what she had said and made sure I conducted myself as a young sixteen-year-old lady should. After all, I realized I was representing my Momma, my family, myself and, most importantly, the Dear Lord.

Reference: "Hold to God's Unchanging Hand"

It Is Well with My Soul

The first Sunday School lesson since the Covid-19 pandemic was on commitment. The writer included the third verse of "It Is Well with My Soul" in the study. I commented that the third verse was often omitted when the song was sung but it was a meaningful verse.

One of the class members stated, "I want that song sung at my funeral."

I said, "Oh, no! We need to give you your flowers while you are living. Let's sing 'It Is Well with My Soul' today."

When we checked our current hymnal, it was not in our book; finally, we were able to locate three old Broadman hymnals that had the song. So I suggested our ten-talent pianist play the song. Her daughter, she, and I would join in for an impromptu special music for the church service today. We shared our idea with the song leader; he was delighted. We decided to sing at the beginning of the service. I shared with the small congregation what prompted our decision to sing today; we began singing two minutes before ten o'clock.

As we sang, nine more people came into church. Amazingly, our unrehearsed presentation of "It Is Well with My Soul" went well—a testimony of the trio's souls' condition.

Reference: "It Is Well with My Soul"

When You Can't Stand...Kneel

While working in healthcare, I learned from my coworkers that one of our precious patients had lost her vision while she was in the hospital. When she returned to the clinic post-hospitalization, I pondered what words to say to her regarding her loss, but none came. I realized she had dealt with poor vision for a number of years but she had her walking-around vision, which meant she had been independent in her own home. Now this loss of vision was potentially quality-of-life changing.

As I cautiously approached her dialysis chair during clinic rounds, I softly called her name and said I was sorry to hear she had a change in her vision while in the hospital. She confirmed what I had been told. "The doctors don't know if my vision will ever improve, but Ina, I have learned that when you can't stand... kneel and that's what I've been doing."

I quickly replied, "That is always the correct action to take, and I will pray for your vision to return, too."

"Thank you," she said.

Thankfully, our prayers were answered, and the precious woman's walking-around vision was restored.

Bloom Where You Are Planted

After I finished a phone call to my older brother to wish him a happy birthday, I started walking back to our cabin. (Yes, I have a cell phone, but I have to stand on the hillside in front of our cabin to get service.) Then something caught my attention. The six irises that I had planted years ago had survived the harsh Kentucky winter. Five of the six had multiplied; one looked like it did the first year that I planted it. No growth at all. Strangely, one of the six clusters of irises had buds. When I counted, there were twenty-three buds on that one section of irises. The remaining five clusters of irises had produced no buds or blooms.

Then the Holy Spirit touched me: "Be sure you are producing buds that will turn into blooms rather than being bloomless."

Years ago, when I moved to Kentucky, a friend gave me a plaque with a small vase in its center that stated "Bloom," which has served as a reminder to bloom where you are planted.

"Thank you once again for the reminder!" I prayed.

Yes, I Believe in God

For years now, I have carried in my Bible a picture of the beautiful smiling face of Cassie Bernall from Littleton, Colorado. Reportedly, the young martyr who attended Columbine High School was asked by the gunman that fateful day, "Do you believe in God?"

When without hesitation she responded, "Yes, I believe in God," the gunman shot her.

Many times I have heard stories of Christian martyrs sacrificing their lives for their faith and prayed that I would be able to do so if called upon to make the ultimate sacrifice but never experienced a situation where remotely this was a possibility until one Sunday my husband and I will never forget.

Our pastor was taking a Sunday off. My husband and I arrived early at church to unlock the door. A young man with long hair who was dressed casually and carried a case arrived next at church. We introduced ourselves to him. In my mind, I thought he might be the speaker our pastor had sent since he did not tell us who he was sending to fill the pulpit in his absence.

The young man told us his name, his car was broken down next door, he had run out of gas, and he didn't have money to buy any gas. He stated he liked to paint; he seemed fascinated by the beautiful stained-glass windows in our small country church.

Other members arrived at the church as well as the association director, who was to be our preacher for the day. As we all talked to the young man, it was apparent he was a troubled young man. Our small congregation dismissed to our Sunday School classes after the opening assembly. The young man went to the men's class.

After Sunday School, the congregation thinned to a handful of people since there seemed to be a concern about the young man's mental health. I continued talking with him, as I wanted him to feel welcomed. I remember my husband whispering in my ear, "Stop talking to him; he is fixated on you!"

During the preaching service, the young man sat near the front of the church; my husband and I sat at the back of the church on our usual pew. Just before the music started, I leaned over to my husband and whispered in his ear, "I know we should leave church today because we don't know what this young man is capable of doing, but I came to church to worship God today, and I'm staying." My husband agreed.

As the preacher delivered God's message for the day, the young man asked questions and made comments that were concerning. At the end of the service, we exited the building to the parking lot. My husband decided to give the young man some money for gas to help him get on his way. When my husband gave the young man the money, he thanked us and said, "You have been kind and good to me; I will see you both again!"

As we drove away from church, my husband and I looked at each other. We both felt it. I can't explain what we felt, but I said, "We will see Him again; in my soul, I feel he was referring to seeing us in Heaven."

We drove the five-minute drive to our farm, ate a quick lunch, and drove past the church on our way to Tennessee. The man's disabled car that had run out of gas was gone. I said, "The small store doesn't have a gas pump. Where did the young man get the gas for his car?" My husband and I were both silent.

Do You Believe in Miracles?

Cindy's Miracle

The same day that I received by mail Guidepost's exclusive offer to preview the books, *It's a God Thing, When Miracles Happen to Everyday People,* and *Do You Believe in Miracles?* I received the weekly local newspaper.

Words cannot describe my thankfulness to God as I read in the newspaper the inspiring story of Cindy's miraculous recovery from Covid-19. Her touching story chronicled the events of the last six months. She stated she believes with all her heart that she survived because God—the great Physician—healed her, her incredible medical team, constant prayers, and her support system.

Last fall, when I was at an estate auction, I asked my brother-in-law how Cindy was doing as she battled Covid-19. He said, "They don't think she will live through the weekend." I was devastated. Even though we had lost track of each other in recent years due to being busy with our children and work as well as attending different churches, I still felt a tremendous connection to her as my sister in Christ. My husband and I continued to pray for her daily; also we added her name to our church's prayer list. On Monday, I felt led to ask one of my dialysis patients (who was a preacher) if he would pray for Cindy's health. I told him she was a dedicated Christian mother and devoted nurse to her patients; I realized all was well with her soul but her passing due to Covid-19 would be a painful loss for her children, patients, and all of us. He agreed to pray for her.

Every day I waited for my brother-in-law to call me. On Thursday, I could no longer stand it. I called him to ask how Cindy was doing. He said, "Unexpectedly, on Monday she started improving and has continued to improve every day since then."

I was so grateful to God that she had survived but continued to pray to God that her health would be restored, recognizing she was facing a long rehab after being bedfast for weeks, but I said, "If anyone can do it, Cindy can!"

I continued to check on Cindy's progress. At the end of December, she left the hospital and went home with her family. What a milestone in her recovery journey that was. Since I had retired from working in dialysis, I asked my supervisor to tell our patient who had prayed for Cindy that she had survived and was home with her family. "Please thank him for praying for her and remind him, as I had discussed with him previously, the day he started praying for her was the day she started improving."

As I read the lovely article written by Cindy and saw her smiling face, I knew "our Cindy" was totally back.

You ask me if I believe in miracles?

"Yes, I do. I just witnessed one!"

Ina's Miracle

Years ago, I went for my routine yearly mammogram. As I waited for the usual letter stating "Normal," I got the unexpected phone call from a nurse stating I needed to come for a "diagnostic mammogram" since something showed up on my routine mammogram. The earliest appointment was ten days out. I agreed to the first available appointment time.

Due to stressful circumstances our family was already enduring, I decided to not tell my husband, family, or friends about my dilemma. Quite frankly, I just didn't want to worry them, but I did talk to the Dear Lord about the situation: "I'm no better than anyone else if I have to go through breast cancer, but with everything else that you already have me doing right now, I just don't understand how I can add having breast cancer to the load. I pray that you remove this mass from me, but if not give me the grace to endure what I must face." I fortified my prayer by adding cruciferous veggies (broccoli, cabbage, and cauliflower) to my diet three times a day. On day nine of my wait, I reached out to a friend that I had known for over thirty years and asked her to pray for my health. She agreed to do so.

As I sat in the waiting room and completed the necessary paperwork for my diagnostic mammogram, the nurse came to the waiting room to talk to me. I said, "The waiting is the stressful part of all this; I need to know something today before I leave."

After the nurse completed my diagnostic mammogram, she smiled and said, "I'm going to walk your results over to radiology to be read."

I said, "How do they look?"

With a smile, she said, "I can't tell you, but I'll get the radiologist to read the results and I'll be right back."

Before she left the room, I said, "May I see the computer screens?"

She said, "Yes."

As I looked at the two computer screens, I noted the first one revealed a green pea-sized mass located next to my ribcage on one of my breasts. The second computer screen (diagnostic mammogram) of the same breast revealed no mass.

I said, "It's totally gone on the second one!"

Smiling, she said, "Let me run these results to radiology so they can read the diagnostic mammogram. I'll be right back!" Minutes later she returned and gleefully said, "All is clear; no further tests needed. See you next year!"

As I floated out of the building, I realized God had healed me. I kept my medical ID bracelet that I wore that day to remind me to be thankful and grateful God healed me. You asked me if I believe in miracles? "Yes, I do! I experienced one!"

Revelation

In life sometimes insight comes through the most unexpected sources. As I watched a TV show where a psychiatrist had been consulted to treat a man's wife who had witnessed the suicide of one of her students whom she had counseled for a year, I was intrigued. The psychiatrist stated, "When you are overloaded, one more thing can tip you over the edge and shut you down." Then the psychiatrist asked the husband about his wife's health before the incident. The husband told the psychiatrist he didn't think his wife had an issue with being overloaded. Then the psychiatrist asked if he noticed her level of anxiety or depression increasing. The husband hesitated and admitted, "Yes, sometimes." Then he asked the psychiatrist how he could tell if his wife was overloaded.

The psychiatrist stated, "I don't view being anxious or depressed as a major sign of being overloaded, but in my opinion, if your joy has left you, you are overloaded."

Oh! I thought. The last few months that I worked in healthcare in the midst of the Covid-19 pandemic, I did my best every day but I realized the joy that I once felt in my heart as I walked across the parking lot to the building was gone. Therefore, I took it as a sign from the Dear Lord that it was time to say goodbye to my job and start a new chapter in my life.

One day as I was scribbling in my Stellar Spiral Notebook, I told my husband, "I realize no one may ever care about the little stories that I am writing, but I feel total joy in my heart as I am writing. Writing makes me happy. Therefore, I am going to continue to record whatever the Dear Lord inspires me to write…."

Epilogue: Milestones

By definition a "milestone" is a pillar or stone set up to show the distance in miles to certain places or important events. When the Dear Lord creates a "milestone" in one's life, one's life becomes changed forever.

Through the little stories in this book, I have shared some of the major "milestones" in my life. I have come to realize "milestones" present opportunities to serve the Dear Lord. When the Holy Spirit inspires our actions, we recognize the actions as ones we probably would not have thought about much less implemented because so often the Holy Spirit's inspired actions require sacrifice, but there is joy in our hearts and peace in our souls when we are doing the will of God!

Thankfully, the Dear Lord placed many encouragers in my life who prayed for me along my life's "milestones." My future "milestones" are in the Dear Lord's capable hands just like they have been all these many years, and so it is with you as well.

As you finish reading these humbly written words in these little stories, please know that I said a prayer for you. May the Dear Lord bless you. May you be drawn closer to His will for your life. If you have not accepted Jesus as your Savior, I pray that you do so; don't delay because without the "milestone" of accepting Jesus as our Savior, nothing else will matter when we bow before the Dear Lord.

References: Ecclesiastes 3:1-2 and Isaiah 45:22-23

ABCs of Salvation

A - Admit you are a sinner. "For all have sinned and come short of the glory of God" (Romans 3:23). "For the wages of sin is death; but the gift of God is eternal life through Jesus Christ our Lord" (Romans 6:23).

B - Believe. "For God So loved the world that he gave his only begotten Son, that whosoever believeth in him should not perish, but have everlasting life. For God sent not his Son into the world to condemn the world; but that the world through him might be save" (John 3:16-17).

C - Confess. "For with the heart man believeth unto righteousness; and with the mouth confession is made unto salvation" (Romans 10:10). "For whosoever shall call upon the name of the Lord shall be saved" (Romans 10:13).

An example of "How to pray to God to become a Christian" (Don't worry if your prayer is not exactly the same as the example; the Dear Lord knows we're not perfect. He knows our hearts and that we are sincerely calling on him to save us from our sins.):

"Dear God, I believe that Jesus is Your Son, that He died on the cross for my sins, and that He was raised from the dead. I ask Jesus into my heart and life; please forgive me of my sins. I accept Jesus as my Savior and Lord; please help me turn away from my sins. Thank you for forgiving me, giving me eternal life, and the hope I now have. In Jesus' name I humbly pray, Amen."

And in obedience to the Lord, be baptized and join a Bible-believing church where you can fellowship with other Christians. By being in the will of God, you will find Joy in your heart and life and Peace in your soul.